Ferment on the Campus

Also by David Mallery

HIGH SCHOOL STUDENTS SPEAK OUT

Ferment

on the CAMPUS

AN ENCOUNTER WITH THE NEW COLLEGE GENERATION

—————————— *by David Mallery*

HARPER & ROW, PUBLISHERS, NEW YORK

70996

Contents

Foreword

College campuses were stirring with student ferment in the early 1960s. The "apathetic" generation had moved on and students then in college were showing interest in national issues and national politics. This seemed a new sort of ferment.

One group of deans of students wanted to make some study of this. There were representatives of western colleges and universities forming the Academic Council of the College Student Personnel Institute (then Western Personnel Institute). For more than thirty years the Institute had, in cooperation with a growing number of member institutions, carried on a changing and expanding program of research, service, and publication in student personnel work.

At the Institute's November 1961 annual conference, the Council's study committee, appointed the year before, was asked to formulate a research proposal, one that would involve listening to students themselves, not to the voices of outside influences.

The resulting proposal was for a study to be made among the Institute's member institutions. The Edward W. Hazen Foundation made a grant available to the Institute in January 1963. The committee sent a memo about the study to all members of the Academic Council asking them to suggest instances of student interest in political and social issues which they were willing to have studied on their own campuses. Seven institutions were chosen, which provided a variety of campus climates. One university was chosen whose difficulties over student political action had been widely publicized. Others had student activities going on usefully without fanfare; some had little to show but were included for contrast.

David Mallery was chosen as director of the study because of his reputation as an accurate reporter who would not impose his own biases between students and readers. This reputation was partially based on his writing in *High School Students Speak Out*, reporting a study he had made for the Committee on School and College Relations of the Educational Records Bureau. In this, the voices of students came through loud and clear, not muffled by the author's opinions. We think David Mallery has done this again in *Ferment on the Campus*.

The visits were made in 1963 and 1964. The Academic Council members read Mr. Mallery's draft report, then discussed it with him and approved it at the Institute's annual conference in November 1964. Mr. Mallery and the committee realized from the start that his report could only be on one period of time and one problem. Another visit to the same campuses would find different situations. Hardly any campus climate remains the same after one dominant student group graduates.

The Institute hopes that circulation of this report will help teachers, college administrators, trustees, and parents to understand better how college students today become interested in major issues of our time.

For the Study Committee:
H. DONALD WINBIGLER
Committee Chairman, and Dean of Students, Stanford University

Byron H. Atkinson, Academic Council Chairman, and Dean of Students, University of California, Los Angeles

Dirck W. Brown, Associate Secretary, National Committee on Teacher Education and Professional Standards, Washington, D.C.; formerly Dean of Students, University of Denver

John C. Clevenger, Academic Council Chairman-elect, and Dean of Students, Washington State University

Donald M. DuShane, Dean of Students, University of Oregon.

Helen Fisk, Committee Secretary, and Institute Editorial Consultant

Arthur H. Kiendl, Headmaster, Mt. Hermon School, formerly Dean of Students, University of Colorado

John T. Palmer, Dean of Students, San Fernando Valley State College

F. Theodore Perkins, Professor of Psychology, Claremont Graduate School and University Center

Arthur L. Tollefson, Associate Dean of Students, California State College at Fullerton, formerly on the staff of College Student Personnel Institute

Jonathan R. Warren, Institute Director of Counseling and Research

John J. Wittich, Executive Director of the Institute

ACKNOWLEDGMENTS

The study committee and the staff of the Institute appreciate help in formulating and planning for the study given by members of the Institute's advisory committee, by Sarah G. Blanding, Paul Braisted, Herbert Gatzke, David Riesman, and Nevitt Sanford. Special thanks go to Harold Taylor who gave impetus to the study at our annual conference in 1961 and who met twice with the study committee.

Ferment on the Campus

1

A New Portrait Taking Shape

Portraits of the "college generation" have been getting painted for many years, and the colors and shapes in the new pictures are as fascinating as the familiar old ones. The painters have always included a great range of observers and commentators from outside and inside the generation in question, as well as the colleges. Rarely have students themselves put in brush strokes, and sometimes the most colorful and sharply defined lines have been drawn by those painters least acquainted with actual, living members of the college generation supposedly serving as models.

The picture emerging right now is of college students on Freedom Rides and picket lines, rallying to the Peace Corps and helping register voters in Alabama, spending the summers tutoring in the slums or building a recreation hall in Uganda, blockading police in the center of campus riots, badgering university administrations for more freedom to organize, to agitate, to serve, to explode. Painters show dedicated students, academically sharper than ever before, identified with the world's problems as never before, seeking out responsibility and maturity through or in spite of their college curriculum and activities. Viewers-with-alarm show wild-eyed hotheads with beards overturning tradition, harassing the authorities, frantically seeking escape from academic and social responsibility in undisciplined brawling on campus and ill-advised meddling off it.

All this is certainly new in relation to the portraits that emerged in the 1950s. It is hard to believe that only ten years ago the college generation sat immobile in the portraits of the time, "the silent generation," cautious note takers, careful in discussion, guarded about the subjects they chose to write papers on, evasive about joining anything, apathetic about politics, hostile to any commitment beyond the books, tests, and papers in their courses and their rather unreported social life.

Back upstairs along the portrait gallery are the pictures of the returning veterans of the forties, bringing a new seriousness and academic intensity to the campuses, and behind them the enthusiastic cause-chasers of the thirties, agitating vigorously about social welfare, discrimination, fascism, military service, and the looming war.

More remote, but flashingly vivid now and then when certain historians show them to us, are the still earlier portraits of college generations. There were those of the mid-nineteenth century American students struggling with increasing force against a faculty determined to educate their minds, purify their souls, work them hard, and guard them from the Devil. Contrasted to these were the portraits of the German students of that same time, living where they wished, moving from one university to another; free men taking and making what they wished out of the experiences of their education. A distinguished ex-college president recently startled a newspaper reporter by reminding him, the day the reporter's paper carried front-page headlines about a massive student riot, that three times before the Civil War, Princeton students had dynamited Nassau Hall, that Yale students around the same time used to enjoy throwing burning coals through the windows of unpopular professors, and that Dartmouth students had a tradition of blowing horns in relays beneath the windows of *their* least favored professors until the poor men packed up and left town. Back yet further, Thomas Jefferson hoped, when he started the University of Virginia in 1825, that it would be "an institution relieved of the historic problems of student uproar." The first months of the University's history evidently dashed these hopes.

Some observers and commentators, bent on showing that nothing ever really changes, reach into Elizabethan times or into the days of Greek glory for a quote about students, and the portrait does have a familiar look. A recent *New York Herald Tribune* column on education quoted some college students and teachers and deans about the campuses of the sixties, and tucked in two comments. The first is from Aristotle, sounding like an echo across 2,400 years:

They [young people] have exalted notions, because they have not yet been humbled by life or learnt its necessary limitations; moreover their hopeful disposition makes them think themselves equal to great things—and that means having exalted notions. They would always rather do noble deeds than useful ones: their lives are regulated more by moral feeling than by reasoning—all their mistakes are in the direction of doing things excessively and vehemently. They overdo everything—they love too much, hate too much, and the same with everything else.

The second is from a student of the sixties, the 1960s, that is:

While at school, modern youth has a last opportunity to accent his idealism. He sees problems in the world and has ideal solutions for them, perhaps drawn from the university, perhaps not. He wants to correct these wrongs now, before he leaves and has to accept the responsibilities of a citizen in a community. So he turns toward some outlet for his idealism—the Student Nonviolent Coordinating Committee, the Peace Corps, etc.—and gives everything he can, even his own life, for a cause. For it is the cause, not his university, that leads him to the crusades into the war against the evils of our society.

The portraits of these students clearly have more in common with the Aristotle portrait than either has with the portraits of the 1950s, in which we saw no sign of exalted notions, of openly expressed moral feeling, of determination to correct wrongs in the society, or of excesses of any kind except possibly in cautiousness. But whatever changes and whatever recurs as not only decades but centuries of college generations succeed each other, the chances are that the portraits painted of them omit many faces, feelings, and complexities in the generation being depicted. Actually, the idea of a *portrait* of a generation implies something that can be seen, fully, at least in two dimensions. More recently the word *profile* has appeared, implying less of a full picture but still some clear lines. Yet those interested in what is actually happening on college campuses too often get only *words* that give the feeling of sweeping description, but which actually do not refer to thousands and thousands of students on the campuses. Perhaps they do not refer directly to any group. Perhaps more than one person cannot sit for a single portrait, and the generalizations that sweep over six million college students in the United States in the 1960s need to be interspersed with, and be affected by, voices, faces, and themes on college campuses today, if they are to give off any honest and helpful light.

As a nation we are fascinated by what these young people are like, but unfortunately we do not agree about the kind of fascination we feel or the kind of influence we want our colleges to have on their students. The new ferment of the sixties is also awakening us to a newer concern: What do we want our college students to *do*, if anything, during their student days, beyond academic work and social play? The only attitude that is shared at all widely when colleges and the college generation are being viewed around the nation is that "A College Education" is a powerful social advantage and a long-range money-earning advantage. Interestingly enough, even those who view the college generation—and their professors—with most alarm still have a powerful respect for "A College Education."

Once we are beyond the point of recognizing our concern, we argue vigorously about colleges and students. Fewer and fewer people take the nostalgic boys-will-be-boys view of the college generation these days. There may be plenty of old grads who still see their own college days as jolly and free and happily uncluttered with responsibility or thought, but their current respect for a college education is coupled with a post-Sputnik awe for the kind of education that can "Beat the Russians." Thus, a growing enthusiasm for hard work has swept the schools from within and without, and has rather automatically included the colleges. More evident is a sense that the college generation is leaving the rest of us behind, outranking us by their new post-Sputnik initiation into technical mysteries, or even by their modern and murky talk about existentialism and alienation, and their still newer talk about commitment and political-social concern. This uneasy feeling brings us to the view that the university should make the students work hard but should not put troubling and controversial ideas into their heads. And if there are a lot of questionable ideas around, launched from the classrooms of troublemaking professors, the students had better keep them inside their notebooks and not start experimenting with them.

Through all this there remains the old and still cherished idea of the college or university as the place where reflection and exploration among ideas and experiences can lead, if not to wisdom, at least to a way of rational thinking and searching and making conclusions, and even to a way of rational behavior. But this composite view immediately splinters into fragments when perceptive individuals begin to ask, *what* experiences, *what* kind of thinking and searching, and, most certainly, *what* ways of behavior? Some groups speak up for the politically militant students of "foreign" universities, students who seat and unseat the nation's government. Others, including those who remind us that our university institutions may not be what we desire them to be, ask for a period of enlightened studenthood in which the student does not have to act by committing himself on social issues and political intensities. "All that can come later," they say. "For now, let the young people study, learn, think, examine alternatives without having to choose up sides." But students attuned to the pace of the times say, "We can't sit on ice indefinitely. 'Later' is just too far away!"

If in this country we listen to so many off-campus voices arguing about colleges and college students, surely we need to hear on-campus voices and to examine some actual behavior of students. It is not just that the figure of six million students is so impressive. Nor is it only because these young people are in that golden spotlight of higher education, blessed by our awe and our concern. The talk about today's college students as "the leaders of tomorrow" has suddenly been compounded by evidence that this generation is displaying some spectacular kinds of leadership *today*.

There are many studies under way of the new college generation, many investigators, and many techniques for examining it. These are not in competition with each other for some prize for *the* definitive portrait, which no study would claim to achieve. The many different ways of approaching the subject may give, as one set of impressions and findings follows another, some real illumination for people in college communities, whether students, professors, administrators, or trustees, as well as for people around the country. All these studies are of importance to those who are interested in the crucial and fascinating subject of higher education itself, and what happens to it and to the six million students who encounter it and each other in the mid-1960s.

This book represents one such study and is the result of some determined and serious searching on the part of a group of college deans. These deans saw the portraits, read the papers, listened to the generalizations. They also saw a lot more than this on their own college campuses. Some saw corroborated there what the public was reading in the papers. Some saw a startling absence of anything like what was supposed to be happening in American colleges and universities from east to west. All saw a picture far more complex, intricate, and interesting than was being offered by and to the commentators and observers off-campus.

The center of the search they wanted to make was *the dynamics of political and social action*. All these deans of students wanted to know more than they saw on their own campuses. What is it like on other campuses? What do students say about their own widening experience in political and social action? How do deans of students and teachers see the new ferment, if in fact it is new? What are some of the things that account for constructive activity on one part of the campus and destructive activity on another part? What experiences on campus and off campus seem to create one or another sort of climate for political and social concern? How is it that there is new ferment on one campus and none on another? How is it that the new interest and activity looks promising and "mature" on one campus and negative and rabble-rousing on another?

These questions never reached the questionnaire stage. They were simply the setting for a series of encounters between a lone investigator and students and adults on seven college and university campuses. The campuses chosen were as different from each other, and in as many ways, as we could find them. We purposely did not choose campuses with the most headlined incidents. We have not used the names of the institutions or the names of any person encountered in them. While there may be readers curious about which college is the subject of discussion, we believe that many readers will find echoes of their own experiences in some of this material and new insights in other parts of it. Thus, these voices may speak for points of view and experiences beyond any one campus, may be of interest and value to readers familiar with many different kinds of college atmospheres.

On each campus the dean of students would line up for the visitor a wide range of conversations with students who had special interests or experiences in the area of political and social action. After these opening conversations, the investigator was on his own, to follow where these conversations led. The dean of students and his staff and the student government were standing by to help arrange for further conversations or to find people who might be particularly helpful in the investigation.

In this report, I was this visitor, and I found the encounters that made up this study a fascinating experience. During the conversations and during the writing of this report, I was determined that there would be many voices heard in this book: voices heard as I heard them, saying what I heard them say to me and to each other. I hope I have been able to do this with justice to the people I talked with, and with helpfulness to people interested in knowing about and "hearing" something direct from college campuses on what issues, what climate, what student, faculty, and administrative ways of behaving seem to make a setting for different kinds of political and social attitudes and action.

I have interwoven my own responses to what I saw and heard, I hope without twisting or blurring the thinking of the people I met. I have read too many studies in which masses of people have been "interviewed," but in which their imagery, their individual style of thinking, has been lost in the flow of the writer's interpretations and philosophizing. I have not kept out of the reporting. I couldn't. The best I could do was to weave together voices, faces, and themes from this experience—and among those voices is my own.

So the portrait painting of the college generation of the sixties is now under way with enthusiasm around the country. If this book does not paint a complete portrait, it may do something more useful: to spotlight individual students and educators, campus intensities and perspectives, that may help our national search for understanding of both what *is* happening on our college campuses and what *should be* happening when professors, deans, and students come together to create the experience of "A College Education" in the world of the 1960s.

2

Havilland College: Ferment in the Middle of the Road

"Climate" is a word that some commentators on college campuses use as if it meant something measurable. Others use it as if it were something mystical that one "breathed" and then understood. Vague as the meaning of the word is, it seems to have strong connotation for students when they are thinking about their own applications of it. Sometimes in one college or university this "campus we know" is very different when described by different ones among the "knowers." So, a visitor's idea of campus climate is going to be a rich mixture of impressions—his own and those of the people he talks with and sees in action. Unless his journeys around campus are extraordinarily well blinkered, he is not going to be very orderly in his view of campus climate, whether he measures it or just "breathes" it.

My encounter with a small college, which I shall call Havilland, examines some of the themes of at least one campus climate. These themes are heard in many variations on the campuses I visited, and the differences in their orchestration and arrangement make for contrasts as striking as when there were differences in the themes themselves. The themes I heard first at Havilland, before anyone got directly onto political and social action, were (1) the inevitable one about student-faculty relationships, (2) the

9

"new" freshmen and the astonishing (to upperclassmen) differences in what they care about and talk about, and (3) the new kinds of interest and talk among students generally. The way these themes develop at Havilland, sometimes bypassing, sometimes interweaving with political and social concerns, was fascinating to discover.

The Dialogue Between Students and Faculty

Of the 1,500 men and women in Havilland College, the most active force for inquiry from among the students was the student chairman of a committee called "Ferment." This committee was charged with responsibility for exploring matters of morale on the campus, including student-faculty relations. "Ferment" had a student chairman and three faculty members on the committee. In talking to me about "Ferment," the chairman launched into the student-faculty theme:

We were concerned about the lack of dialogue between students and faculty—it's rare that even the men and women on campus get to talk things over together and even rarer that student and faculty talk seriously together outside the classroom. The first meeting we had was on "Can we control human behavior?" We had five discussion groups of ten students each, in faculty homes, all on the same night. Some of the groups had two or three professors in them. We had discussions on the aesthetic of music and jazz . . . legalized abortion . . . it was interesting to hear girls—I have no sisters—talk about virginity and sexual morals. It was interesting, too, to hear the chaplain talk about *his* generation and the attitude his contemporaries had about these things when they were in college. All this was fascinating. And it's the kind of thing we never would get without an organized setup like this.

He spoke about the faculty's part in this venture.

The biggest drag is the lack of interest among the professors. We want the mainstays among the faculty—like my department chairman who just won't be drawn out *ever* in any kind of conversation. Of course there are always the campus gadflies—they'll always come—but we want the people who are more entrenched in the college to take part in these things. My department man, for instance, is fascinated by the idea of power and politics and he is a big man in the church. I'm getting very interested in religion and I'm a political science major. I'd love to hear how he talks about these two special interests, but I can't get him engaged in any kind of conversation about it. But we have to settle for what we can get. For instance, in one of these groups talking about, "Can we control human behavior?" there was an existentialist teacher and a determinist teacher. It was fascinating to watch the two of them go at each other.

As I had seen on other campuses, almost any talk about the "new" intellectual thrust came around to the "new" freshmen. Juniors and seniors would so often take a fatherly view of the incoming freshmen, and often they saw them almost with awe. The "Ferment" chairman brought his college's "new" freshmen into the conversation just at the point where he was warming up to the fascination of watching professors with conflicting views have a go at each other.

The freshmen are right in the middle of all this. For one thing, we see to it that they get into the swim. We have them read B. F. Skinner's *Walden Two* and two or three other books over the summer, and I also see to it that we have a place in the library which has reading matter for the "Ferment" groups—books and articles that students are supposed to read before they come. About fifty students were involved in this evening that we had. Also half of the teachers involved this year were new to these groups, and twelve of the solidly entrenched faculty said they couldn't come this time but they'd like to come next time—that they were genuinely interested. Even in the language department there was interest. This is a real sign of progress! We planned a discussion on Civil Rights, the arts, and the Dean suggested a good one—the gulf between the generations. Then there's this big powwow coming up—the Kennedy Years, a Student Appraisal. We're going to have students from most western states and some eastern.

This student had started in on faculty-student relationships, but that subject was clearly a part of what he saw as a new interest, a new enthusiasm for exciting, nonclassroom talk about ideas, values, about controversy itself. There was no question in his mind that this was "new," an answer to the talk about apathy that he said he used to hear about in school when people talked about college campuses.

This kind of interest never would have happened when I was a freshman. It's unthinkable. Yet now it's a big thing on the campus. I think our class marks the change, a real social concern now and religious concern. There's a dynamic new chaplain here, incidentally. The kids are reading Niebuhr and Tillich—you never would have heard this sort of thing discussed four years ago.

He went on to speak of a professor of philosophy who was setting up issues and encouraging controversies that were being fought out in the dormitories, and a new course in twentieth century ethics to which political science, economics and science majors were flocking.

Apathy had been such a favorite topic for so long, in any analysis of campus climates, that I asked if it had just disappeared here at Havilland. It had clearly not disappeared from some of the other campuses. The chairman of "Ferment" thought a moment and then said:

I think there's a level of interest over the whole top of the campus. There's probably a lot of dullness and apathy underneath this level of interest. The interest is what shows, though. Or maybe it's just that I'm seeing the whole thing with rose-colored glasses. No—I'll tell you this: it's not just a question of pockets of enthusiasm and interest in a sea of dullness. It's pockets of dullness in a sea of interest!

He jumped to some examples of the "sea of interest":

I'm a freshman advisor in a dorm, and you should hear the things the freshmen discuss seriously. You ought to hear them talking about Plato while they're shaving at 6:30 A.M.! We never used to do that, but we do it now. We used to degenerate into sex. They don't. Or at least it takes them longer to!

Asked for some of the reasons for this interest that he felt covered the whole campus, he spoke of a freshman history course:

There's a lot of talk among freshmen about the History of Civ course. It's required, and it's really potent. But it's more in the air than just in one freshman course. For instance, my roommate is a chemistry major. He spent most of his four years with his test tubes, but now he's suddenly come out. He went to our session on 'Can we control human behavior?' and he's just signed up for a philosophy course. This is the kind of thing I mean. . . .

This fellow may have been so elated at all the intellectual interest and excitement he found around and within him that he went overboard in ascribing it to so many of the Havilland students. Yet this was just the kind of young man who, it seemed to me, would have been most agonized in the midst of the silent-generation-apathy about which we used to hear from college campuses. I don't think he ever would have been comfortable in it. He would have been clamoring for something more. And at Havilland in 1964, he was getting it. Surely, this interest and excitement about ideas, values, and beliefs was a powerful force in the life of a campus. One can imagine the enthusiasm aroused in a classroom when even a handful of students brings this spirit instead of the "old" careful note taking and guarded class participation. This spirit puts demands on the professor. It challenges him as a human being as well as a scholar. He is drawn into out-of-class conversations and forums where he cannot simply lecture and dominate. And he is at least invited to commit himself to his own beliefs and concerns in ways that the "old" climate did not ask of him.

This new intellectual curiosity also extends new challenges to the student personnel staff. The "Ferment" chairman's roommate, who had spent almost all his four years with test tubes, must have been an easier person to have around after he had "awakened" in that last half-year and asked a lot of questions and chased after their answers.

Some intellectual talk among students can be "safe," and some can be incendiary. Students don't have to join CORE or go to Mississippi or Africa in order to make a dent on the thought and behavior of a college campus. This new questioning and probing from students can make new problems for the traditional keep-the-lid-on type of dean, but also can create new opportunities for enterprising personnel people who see themselves as educators and not Dutch uncles.

Perhaps most promising are the implications of this new spirit in student life, for we have heard a long time about the deadening effects of the student peer culture and here we see possibilities for counteracting it. Freshmen arriving on campus having already gone through some highly provocative reading over the summer, standing by the shaving mirror and hearing the talk the "Ferment" chairman described about Plato or Niebuhr, seeing and hearing some professors in action as men and women, off the rostrum as well as on it, walking into this kind of human questioning and digging in dormitories, dining halls, and student unions. Experiences like these can surely redefine what education is to a young man or woman. The millenium may not have come all at once to Havilland, but the kind of enthusiasm this young man was talking about, crucial to his experience of the campus climate, certainly changes the experience of teaching in a college, of administering a college, and of going to college.

Politics: A Communist Speaker or a Million Dollars?

Politics was part of this new excitement and new talk at Havilland, though often it was not the same people who were excited about politics as were excited about Tillich or religious ethics courses or student-faculty discussions about legalized abortion. And on political matters, the students and professors did not seem to be talking together. They were talking across a great deal of empty space to each other, if they talked at all. The main political focus at Havilland was on getting permission to have Communist speakers on campus. On many campuses this focus seems to be an early stage of political awareness among the students. Students on more active and politically sophisticated campuses might smile at this focus, though some states and some boards of managers still have fixed rules about Communist speakers, and these are red flags to students, regardless of their political sophistication.

At Havilland the feeling seemed to be that students who cared about political questions were insulted at the thought that they should be insulated from ever hearing or seeing a real live Communist. On a campus as middle-of-the-road and as short on extremists as this one was, there still was a feeling that "we should be allowed to hear the other side—it's a matter of intellectual honesty, of academic freedom."

An American Communist Party official was to come to speak on campus in two weeks. The dean of students had made clear to the students that "the college welcomes free inquiry, and this includes controversial speakers. The college asks that the issues be relative to the education of the student and that the inquiry be carried on responsibly." The campus Young Republicans and the Young Democrats jointly sponsored the speaker, who was to discuss civil liberties in the United States and in Soviet Russia. A 45-minute speech was planned, with a 45-minute question period. No one seemed to expect much from the speaker, for evidently he had a reputation for dullness, wafting from campus after campus. It was just "the principle," as one student said, "the fact that we don't have to be protected and coddled as if the first thing we heard that wasn't true blue would make us sign up in the C.P. or take the first plane for Moscow."

The response that most shocked students was clearly that of one of the most respected and stimulating political science professors, who said about the coming speech, "Do you realize that this speech will cost the college about one million dollars in donations?" I was used to hearing from students that "the administration," or "the dean," or "the president," or "the trustees," or "*they*" were wary of financial losses to the college or mud on the college image if objectionable speakers were brought on campus. But this was the first time that I had heard students quote, in distress, an admired faculty member with such an attitude. The dean of students said simply: "This is a matter of students breathing fresh air . . . being allowed to operate responsibly and in freedom on these things." Yet even he saw with some apprehension the conflicting and emotion-ridden thrusts of this "first" with some other firsts, particularly in a mushrooming interest among students in participation in civil rights demonstrations. "The issues can get blurred," the dean said to me, "and the irresponsible students can get into the picture and then it all gets murky."

A *Principle, Not a Speaker*

The student who was head of the Political Science Forum at
Havilland tried to throw some light on why the coming speech was
such a "first":

> The Political Science Forum has always been pretty passive—so has
> student interest in political things. But interest began to boil up in the
> spring of '63 when we brought in some local political people to talk
> for short sessions. These were candidates for local offices, mostly. But
> the trouble was, our students have trouble functioning in this kind of
> situation. They go shy, or they don't know what questions to ask. I
> think we lack here a real group of red-hot liberals. That kind of spirit
> is developing a little bit here and there, but it's nothing compared, say,
> to Berkeley.

Whenever I was talking, on any of the campuses, with the most
dedicated and active students, particularly those concerned with
politics or civil rights, Berkeley shone forth as the mecca of student action, a kind of ideal of concern for political and social
matters against which other campus intensities and activities could
be measured. Yet I was to hear some awe and horror of Berkeley
students expressed by other men and women on Havilland's campus, evoked mostly by myths and realities about beards and bath-
ing rather than red-hot liberalism.

The Forum student spoke at length of the political science professor and the warning of the loss of a million dollars to Havilland:

> I just can't see how he sees this thing. He said, "Why didn't we go
> the week before and get a stripper from the Pink Pussy Night Club
> and bring her here to talk about stripping?" This would make sense to
> him, he said, in the same way as having the Communist Party man
> would make sense to him. I just can't see it. I think this view will
> make some trouble, though. It may divide the dean of students, who
> has supported this thing, and his followers from the political science
> man and his.

The most interested students and the dean of students seemed
to have an almost clinical attitude toward the coming speech.

There was a principle being acted out, and it made sense. Even the rumors of students in the background capitalizing on the coming event for their own renown did not seem to detract from this principle. The political science man's attitude was seen far more as something painful, confused, and confusing rather than as something against which to rally the troops. It seemed clear that the student leaders at Havilland were not engaged in some kind of antiauthority agitation in their eagerness for *the fact* of the coming speech. There must have been enough antiadult ferment in the background to cause concern to the dean of students about "the murkiness," but the students who were carrying the ball maintained this clinical attitude, a kind of detachment from the speaker's subject, along with a commitment to the importance of his being permitted to come.

Where Are the Extreme Ones?

Fresh from talking with New Conservatives at Mountain University and Young Socialists at City University, I asked the student head of the campus Young Democrats why Havilland didn't have the range of intensities in political matters that some of the other colleges and universities had. He answered:

I think that those who aren't apathetic here tend to be realistic. A real extremist would have trouble finding a partner in a campus this size, or on this campus, anyway. There's a tradition here for voicing political views, quite a variety of them, within one or another group. Our Y.R.'s and Y.D.'s include quite a variety of attitudes within each. At the big places there are really wild fringe groups with enough people to make a little unit of each. Also it may be that we're not all that exciting here, or excited.

He knew a good deal about campus fringe groups in other universities, and I asked him about these.

I've visited the whole range of them, fifty-four of them, extreme right and extreme left. I'm even worried about being seen at some of them, but I can prove that I've been at the whole range and not just one kind. The trouble with all these extreme groups is that they're *unrealistic*. They are loaded with negative rebellion. They want to get rid of things, but they have no constructive approach to substitute. They have nothing to get out and *do*.

Here was one of the most politically conscious students on campus, whose interest, like most of his politically minded friends, was more clinical than activist. His study of the fifty-four political groups was evidently a fascinating project for him because he was interested in the way people thought about politics, whether left, right, or center. But the intensities that he saw in the groups he was studying were not to be found at Havilland. This absence of passion in the political dialogue on campus did not seem a serious lack to most of the students I talked with. They prided themselves on seeing *objectively*—a magic, almost sacred word to so many students on these campuses—of wanting to listen, learn, explore, study political ideas and behavior with energy and enthusiasm, all "above" the intensities of the extremes in the spectrum or in behavior.

The dean of students and others on the faculty and administration seemed to think there was quite enough intensity in all the noise about getting a Communist speaker and in the stirrings to get a CORE chapter on campus. Yet students on some of the other campuses I visited would have smiled to hear some of this rather removed, analytical talk. They would have said that some of these Havilland students lacked *involvement, commitment*, real dedication to a political position. These Havilland students with special political interests would have answered that by their objectivity, their effort to seek out ideas and have them aired and examined, they were doing the student's job, were *learning*, were using their student days in the way they should be used. Dedication to a political group or cult or action project would seem to these people perhaps a rather naïve approach, a way of losing sight of a highly complex and interesting forest that was there to be explored, tree by tree. The real dedication, the real involvement of the individual student, appeared at Havilland not so much in political matters as in international concerns and experiences of service, on a personal basis, whether in Africa or down the street.

An International Emphasis

"The world" reached into Havilland's climate in matters that were not directly political. The college had a strong history of interest and a lot of student participation in international concerns. These concerns were not necessarily nonpolitical or anti-political. Again, the students with the international interests, mainly related to *people,* were different from those in the political activities, mainly related to issues, or, at the moment, *the* issue of lifting the ban on Communist speakers.

The most forceful spokesman for international interests was not surprisingly the head of the International Club. Yet his comments about the Club and about the campus itself reached way beyond simple meetings and activities. His view of what the college's international emphasis meant, in and beyond his own academic experience, was something that made clear to me another major theme in the climate of Havilland College:

The International Club is an outlet for me . . . some people just grind it out in their classes. They never read papers. They just go for the grades. The organizations aren't a big help—the Y.R.'s and the Y.D.'s and the Havilland Christian Fellowship. The I Club will have a lot of different kinds of programs and different kinds of people will show up at different ones. Tonight we're having six students showing slides from their travels, people from the Experiment in International Living, the Havilland European trip, the Havilland Asiatic tour, etc. There's real interest in travel . . . "How do I get abroad? What are the mechanics, financing?" . . . all that.

Like most of the students I had met who had a special interest or dedication, he had found his long before coming to college. "I was always interested in travel. I went to Europe with my family when I was very young. I went through half of my senior year in high school in Heidelberg. I did this on my own—I sold my surf board and built a bank account!" His international experiences were important to him: the half-year in school in Heidelberg, nine weeks on his own in Mexico when he was fourteen, considerable exploration on his own in Spanish and Latin American affairs, a growing interest in Japanese studies. In fact he seemed so stimulated by all this that I wondered if Havilland or any campus might not seem to him as flat and provincial. It clearly did not, and for him and some other internationally minded students I met, the relationships with foreign students on campus was a major part of *why* it did not.

This young man spoke of the "whole new element in my life here at college" in his relationships with foreign students. Again and again I would hear at Havilland about how "uniform" the student body seemed to be: " . . . upper middle class, pretty heavy on materialism, the labels on the sweaters, the cars, you know. . . ." Although self-conscious about what they saw as uniformity, these internationally minded students were grateful for the reality of an African student down the hall, a boy as ablaze as his nation with the idea of national independence, or a Japanese girl in the next room whose family remembered well the bombings of 1944 and 1945 in their city.

One student put it this way: "In the academic sense, the work here is more than adequate. Yet there's a longing to get out of the academic and go ask some kid from Iran or Ghana or Japan what he feels about United States air bases or nuclear tests. . . ." There had been what some students spoke of as a tremendous discussion two nights before in the Student Peace Union on the dropping of the atom bomb on Hiroshima and Nagasaki. It had come up quite spontaneously, and students had gradually joined in, with the word spreading across the campus that there was something exciting going on in the conversation in the Union. And the foreign students, not only those from Japan, were what gave "a sense of reality," as one student called it, to the supposedly "uniform" Havilland students.

This sense of reality, a genuine human exchange with the foreign students, struck me as a significant achievement at Havilland. In other schools and colleges, one hears of foreign students sometimes in relation to "how they're just like us," how they fit in, play football, sing, drink with the fellows. The satisfaction seems to be in that "we're all alike." Then there are the schools and colleges that seem pulled into a kind of self-consciousness about featuring national differences in surface ways, what one student called "the tell-us-all-about-your-folk-dances" approach. At Havilland, the internationally minded students, those from the United States and from other countries around the world, appeared to be conversing with each other in a way that mattered, or at least that mattered to the Americans. Such conversation gave them a sense of reality in international affairs that they could not get, they said, alone in high-powered academic study. Of course this experience is still *talk*, just as the new enthusiasm for ideas at the dormitory shaving mirrors and the drive for a Communist speaker were *talk*. But talk of this kind is certainly experience, and it is not empty simply because there is no action beyond the talk, no constitution, petition, or parade.

Yet, for others on campus, this talk was not enough. For still others, it was not anything. They didn't even know about it or take part in it if they did know, although many of them had international concerns of their own, centered in the feeling of service, though students were wary of that word. The interest in *doing something* physically, beyond talk and study and exploration, led such students along a different road from that of the International Club president and his friends. The theme was still generally "international relations" when I talked with four students a few hours later, three of them just back from a summer with Crossroads Africa and clearly electrified by the experience. Theirs was a major personal revelation, and the revelation seemed to illuminate their own selves as well as their own vision of international relations. They all agreed that the first presentation to the campus by Dr. James Robinson in his explanation of Crossroads Africa had had a dramatic impact on many key people and groups at Havilland. Yet, one said, "Most of the students here have some impulse when they come here—the impulse to *do* something, to be idealistic, to get out and work, to see new things. But it's unchanneled. There's a fragmentation of interests here. Everybody's a specialist whether it's in Toulouse Lautrec or jazz."

They felt that whatever the students brought with them to the campus, Dr. Robinson's speech did suddenly light up some of these idealistic impulses. One student spoke for many of those I had met on this and other campuses when he said, "He really kicked us nicely, in the way we wanted to be kicked. People want a new frontier. They want a sense of there being a couple of trees to cut down and a cabin to build. They don't want the soft way. They don't want to go in soft cars. They'll settle for bicycles."

The whole question of selfishness and motives for service got a vigorous shaking from these students. One young man said with some force, "In Africa we discovered quick enough that we had *no* material contribution to make. That wasn't the point of our going." Another, who had not been to Africa, answered him: "Well, another thing is you're helping develop human minds in a sports club with underprivileged kids. What could be more important than that? That's doing something for somebody." One of the girls agreed, yet added another dimension to the argument:

We had a man from the Peace Corps here. He talked all about the glory and the United States flag in the breeze, and gave us the real hard sell on the thing, and it was terrible. There's all kinds of meanings to idealism. The kind that really counts is not the kind that tells you you're going out to conquer the world, but the kind that says you're going out to cope with a problem and develop yourself in doing it. You have to be adjustable. You have to be willing to take yourself apart and put yourself together again. It's not our building of the school that did this for me. It's the whole world view that I had that was changed.

These students knew that something important had happened to them, something so major that they saw themselves as being entirely different from what they were before the experience. The challenge, and fun, of coming back to shatter some stereotypes at home and at Havilland was part of their shaping of this new self. It was not simply the experience in Africa. The remolding was continuing as they tried to describe what they'd done, what had happened to them, what they wanted their families and their college friends to think about, to understand. These students were not just a tiny, off-beat minority at Havilland. "Everybody" had not gone to Africa in the past summer, but the climate that led to their and others' going—and to their careful language about idealism and service, self-development, and personal relationships, their old and the new selves—seemed to them to be congenial to a lot of the thought and feeling on this campus.

Never once did I hear the word "extra curricular" from a Havilland student. The term may be disappearing from even educators' talk as more and more of what one student called "the busy activities stuff" is falling into disrepute, and the nonclassroom experiences (whether in talk or in doing) that remain count so heavily for students that they can't be called "extra" anything. What impresses a visitor at Havilland is not that there are nonclassroom talk and concern about ideas, beliefs, and personal and international interests, but rather that these activities have such vitality, that they count so much in what students think is important to their education, *and* are not unrelated to some of the best classroom experiences. Students sometimes rather easily assume that nothing in the curriculum "matters."

A nostalgic view of college, which we had heard for years since the novels of Fitzgerald, is that nothing important ever happened in a classroom, that the courses and professors were totally irrelevant to the important experiences students were having in college. There are plenty of students who still feel this way, if I am to judge by what I have seen and heard in this study, but I heard less of it at Havilland, and heard more positive comment about the relation of courses and professors to the talk, at least, that mattered to students. This surely is an aspect of campus climate worth paying attention to.

The most revealing analyses of the conversations described in this chapter came from three students and a chaplain, each of whom *did* feel somehow that he was one of a kind of struggling minority on campus. They saw some of their interests reaching out even to the lab, the library, and the isolated room mate, and it is in this sense that their view of Havilland, described in the next chapter, added a new dimension to what I was to understand about the climate of that college.

3

Climate at Havilland:
Private Service, Public Talk,
New Caring, Old Caution

"If you want to find out about the prevailing convictions on a campus about religion, politics, social service, civil rights, social justice, and all the rest, the place you *don't* go to find out is the Y office or the Christian Club, the Young Presbyterians, or Young Episcopalians. They are already committed, by idealism, by conviction, by compulsion, or by neurosis." Among the "thoughts for the day" that I heard from college administrators and teachers before starting in on this study, this one stuck in my mind rather uncomfortably. I couldn't forget it, even as I talked with some of the most impressive students in just such groups. Yet small pockets of intense conviction, of real concern, *can* have real influence, *can* be actually powerful forces on a campus or in a society, for good or for bad. And these same pockets of conviction, even if they do not light up a campus or society, may be working in more persuasive and pervasive ways, in and beyond their own community, to accomplish more than simply the nourishment of the concerns (or nurturing the obsessions) of a small collection of dedicated people.

Havilland's Christian Fellowship group may be just the sort of thing my friend would have said to stay away from or to listen to warily. Yet my encounter with a few of them told me that there was something here of real importance for college students, teach-

ers, and administrators to listen to with some care. For here were
a few voices, and a few thrusts of concern, that had a great deal to
do with campus climate at Havilland.

The group I met included a young man who was student head
of the Christian Fellowship, two young women who were active in
it, and the chaplain. There was a confident, mutually trusting
relationship between the students and the chaplain, a relationship
that is worth noting in the midst of all the talk one hears about the
impossibility of communication between adults and today's college generation. These three students wanted to influence their
campus, to reach out to as wide a range of student interests as
they possibly could. The Fellowship's chairman made this clear:

There are going to be only a few people who can participate in the
worship aspect of the thing. More will want to have a part in the
service aspect. Still others will want to be in the intellectual-question-
ing aspect, and maybe others will want a part in the social action
aspect. We try to get a lot of people involved in one or maybe two of
these aspects of Fellowship's work. . . .

The students plunged into an analysis of the Havilland attitudes
toward religion. The college, they felt, included a good many students who came because of Havilland's church relationship and
who were reacting against just the church beliefs that had at-
tracted them or their parents to Havilland in the first place. As
one student put it, "They say they're not about to buy all this
church jazz, but they are products of it." The chaplain made this
comparison:

That, you see, is very different from the very secular assumptions of
a university like City. Religion is like a breath of fresh air there and
the chaplain is very pleased with his role there. Here it's very different
—the students talk a lot about how they are resisting "all that church
jazz," but it's in the background of the three-quarters of them who are
Protestant.

The C.F. Reaches Out

Havilland's Christian Fellowship, "C.F.", had been until recently on the defensive against a campus image of fundamental-

ism, piety, and rigidity. "We haven't had that kind of attitude *in* the group," one of the girls insisted, "but even the words 'Christian Fellowship' seemed to lick us before we could start, with most of the students." The other girl introduced a key theme in the changing pattern of Havilland attitudes toward religion: "It used to be almost as if you had to apologize for having any beliefs at *all*. You had to defend yourself on all the beliefs they *thought* you had, but which you *didn't* have."

This attitude was clearly shifting. When I was on the campus, a theologian was just ending a week's visit to Havilland. As these and other students referred to this man's impact, I began to see something of the changing attitudes, even within the C.F., and certainly on the campus as a whole. The C.F. students who were intelligently and exploratively in the middle of dorm conversations and question periods about the visiting theologian's speeches and seminars seemed to do the cause of Christian Fellowship some good on campus. Questioning, inside and outside of C.F., was the thing. I had heard plenty of this from other students, but it came strongly from within the C.F. and from students talking eagerly about religion. Students seemed reassured that they could question religious beliefs and positions even with supposed believers.

Apparently the more usual pattern is for nonbelievers and sharp questioners simply to bait believers. This seems to lead to a division in which the nonbelievers and the believers each talk only among themselves and see each other as closed-minded clods. Still more important, at Havilland those suspicious of organized religion or suspicious of belief itself could not only get more and more into useful *talk* with people who were closer to a manageable set of religious convictions. They could also *work* with them in the social service projects that C.F. and a few other campus organizations sponsored. Here, again, the professor's warning, quoted at the beginning of this chapter, did not apply to Havilland. The supposed fuddy-duddies and do-gooders were not cut off from the skeptical intellectuals. Social concern did not become the province of "those already committed, by idealism, by conviction, by compulsion, or by neurosis."

Talk

The nature of the talk and of the service projects was particularly interesting. The visiting theologian evidently arrived on a wave of campus discussion about religion, and he rode it skillfully—but he also changed it. He intensified what one student referred to as "the constant Ping-Pong game of ideas around here." Some students wouldn't have liked the use of the word "game" here. Others would say that was just the right word and that they loved the game. The essential part seemed to be that the game should not involve one emotionally. A C.F. student said that the question he heard more than any other on campus was, "Have you got any *intellectual* basis for that?" Along with this would come the scoffing about "thinking with the emotions," and "getting lost in value judgments."

The beauty of the visiting theologian's contribution appeared to be that he crossed the boundaries of religion, psychology, anthropology, sociology, and philosophy in a way that made his and the subsequent student discussions acceptably analytical, even academic. Students outside the C.F. found it reassuringly objective to hear the *vocabulary* of these various disciplines coming from the lips of a theologian. People of the C.F. frame of mind were pleased because values and beliefs dear to them were being discussed seriously, regardless of vocabulary. One said:

This man's got us discussing the human situation—got us discussing what we think of ourselves. And he's won the people who are committed to some objective approach. Around here it's the thing to be "oriented toward" philosophy or psychology or anthropology or some particular angle. The *least* acceptable is religion, but I notice everybody's mighty glad to talk about religion, provided they don't have to use religion's language!

The Ping-Pong game of ideas was also intensified by the History of Civilization course, which took one-third of the course time of students' first two years. The teachers of the course came from humanities, sociology, science, and the arts. Not only was this crossing of boundaries exciting to students, but also it allowed for a new perspective on religion. A student said, "We know which professors are churchgoers. Some of the top science men are, for instance. And we know about some of the philosophy and psychology—and even religion—teachers who are not." The chaplain added to this, "I must admit that it seems to me that the physical scientists are the most modest in this matter of belief. The arrogant ones around the teaching profession in colleges and universities seem to be in the social sciences and the humanities— arrogant, that is, in their negativity. The physical science people are humbled by their own methodology." One of the students summarized this by simply saying, "Well, it all makes plenty of lively speculation in and out of class. It adds to the excitement of the talk around here."

The Service Part

The C.F.-sponsored service projects were now drawing those students around the campus who were neutral or even hostile to their image of C.F. attitudes. The college was running several tutorial programs. One was for high school dropouts, many of Mexican background. Others involved much younger children. There was real eagerness about these experiences. Interestingly enough, the high school dropout program was not directly sponsored by C.F. The group felt it would be better not to be identified with the vestiges of the "old" aura of C.F. But C.F. launched it with a powerful set of introductory programs.

There were other service projects in nearby bad-housing areas, in which college students painted and plastered alongside the people who lived in the area. One of Havilland's graduates had returned from Yale Divinity School and had organized a plan by which Havilland students worked with groups of five children each. Each student had his own five children from eight to ten years old, and spent about half of each Saturday with them on walks, games, trips around the city, sports, reading, and talk. The students taking part in this had tripled in number in the current semester. Still another tutoring program involving eight Havilland students had been launched in one of the nearby elementary schools described by a C.F. member as "people who would never touch C.F. with a ten foot pole." Still others engaged in regular sessions with blind children and adults at the Braille Institute. Then there was the Crossroads Africa enthusiasm, referred to in the preceding chapter, in which some of the same spirit was abounding. The chaplain spoke of an almost uncontrollable enthusiasm when the Negro pastor from Harlem came to describe his vision of a person-to-person program bringing Americans and Africans together. "He came here and took the students up that hill to our Greek theatre like a Pied Piper, and absolutely galvanized them."

Whether dramatically launched, or more quietly worked out, these service experiences counted heavily on this campus in the minds of a good many more students than those arriving at Havilland with a full-blown case of social concern. And the rationale, even the style, of those involved beyond the C.F. nearly always seemed to be in the spirit of the student described to me by the young man who said, "These things snowball. Someone will come in and have to show his credentials of being a slob. Then he'll volunteer. One guy came in to the C.F. office last month and said, 'Look, I think everything you people do is great. It's just that I haven't got any compassion!' Now he's in the tutoring work with the high school dropouts every Saturday!"

The C.F. students active in service projects were happy to stop arguing motives and to focus on service. Like the Crossroads Africa students I had met earlier, they saw the futility of too much analysis of, "Why am I doing this?" or "Is it to help others or to broaden myself?", and similar angles in that whole circle of questions. One girl had to get in a last word about motives however, and chose "concern" as the safest word to use. She had been talking about student projects with the American Friends Service Committee in mental hospitals and institutions for retarded children:

All these service projects are not just a study thing. Our psychology department is interested in some of them for the study thing, but the main motive is *concern*. One day in a mental hospital or even twenty Saturdays tutoring some kid may not sound like much, but the *con-*

cern is important and I don't see why we should be so squeamish about saying so.

The Chaplain: "What is Missing?"

When I talked with the chaplain alone, he brought up a kind of concern the C.F. students, and even the politically alert students, had minimized. This was what the chaplain called "the public side of social action." The term *social action* was used little by students I met, or if it was used, it referred to service projects such as those just mentioned. "Social action" has recently come exclusively to mean picketing, marching, and demonstrating to many people. The chaplain was concerned that that area of social action was missing at Havilland. He described the students as "people who say they can't buy this whole Christian thing and can't prove the church's position intellectually, but they 'kind of like' the Christian ethic—being fair and just and honest—and they like compassion." This seemed to the chaplain to provide some ground for social action, but what resulted was private service experiences and almost a conscious turning away from the public side.

There was little evidence here of the kick-up-a-fuss approach to political and social concerns. The chaplain couldn't find any real excitement for public protests in "the public affirmation of identity with people who are being stepped on—like the Negroes—who need support." He had hoped, in the new wave of talk and service at Havilland, to see students reading papers, looking for problems to relate to in the community and the nation, making noise, being heard. But thus far there had only been the personal, private service experiences. He did speak of some student interest in developing a CORE chapter. There seemed to be some apprehension about this, not because of CORE so much as because of the type of student who was agitating for it at Havilland. Other faculty members and some students seemed wary of these elements as well. The chaplain would have been overjoyed to see some of the top C.F. leaders seize the idea of starting a CORE chapter:

This would have been a way for us to be *related* to a major issue. But our best people tend to be squeamish about this kind of commitment. We have the kind of school which could let the whole Mississippi explosion come and go and then, well after it was over, would start drawing up a petition about it.

It may be that Havilland students' tutoring of deprived Negro children counts for more than a march of the same students carrying placards past an all-white housing development. The chaplain admitted this, and called it "creative grub work," a positive effort to have a part in the massive educational effort needed to bring the Negro up to the level "where he can exploit his legal equality." And if the best of Havilland's concerned students were timid about public positions and public actions, they were far from apathetic about *their kind* of social action—the individual, person-to-person service that seemed to mean so much to a surprising number of students. At Havilland, those who were beginning to agitate on the *public* side of social action were those the chaplain spoke of as "people I'll have to watch out of the side of my eye as I march with them."

4

Mountain University:
A Political Explosion

The crisis of the university described here may seem old by the time this study reaches print. It is true that Mountain University today has a new administration, new interests, and new students, and it has for over a year been out of news headlines. Nevertheless this story needs telling. College students, teachers, and administrators in the 1960s are far from immune to the kind of ordeal that wracked this university. An examination of the ordeal here may be helpful to an understanding of how students can perceive the experience of a campus under political attack: how they may identify with it, watch it, misinterpret it, try to ignore it, and as some of Mountain University's students clearly show, how and what they may learn by it.

The Setting

By April 1963, the University, with a student body of 11,500, had just been through a major upheaval, climactic stages of which were exploding from March 1962 on. Though I never introduced the subject, this experience was at the center of many of the conversations I had with students. However the ordeal may have been viewed, understood, or interpreted, it was *the* social-political issue on campus. A quick factual description is needed here to show something of the intensities sweeping this campus, intensities

32

to which students were reacting with strong emotion or dazed confusion, with bitter cynicism or uncomfortable detachment, or a sense of promise and hope.

Any outsider's summary of such an extraordinarily complex, emotion-charged experience as this one will be ridiculously inadequate to those who saw it from inside. Yet there are some major events, with whatever background in other events, feelings, personalities, and local and national political winds, which are readily apparent to any observer.

"The Liberal Dynasty"

Well before the beginning of the climactic period of spring 1962, spokesmen in the community, the legislature, and the University itself were charging the University's president and his administration with "left-wingism," "favoritism to liberal professors," (usually "outsiders"), "brainwashing students," "autocracy, and "administrative inefficiency." Students and faculty were subjected to charges of "radicalism" and "immorality." The controversy moved more and more into the center of the political arena, since the University's president, a former Democratic mayor of a nearby city, and a university regent, up for re-election on the Republican ticket, became focal points in a bitter struggle.

In the spring of 1962, Senator Barry Goldwater of Arizona made a speech on campus in an auditorium filled with over 3,000 students. There was some heckling and picketing by members of the Young People's Socialist League, a group of some twenty students on campus. The nature of this heckling was debated intermittently in the subsequent months. Some saw it as inoffensive and of little signficance. Others saw it as insulting and sinister. The student newspaper published articles hostile to the Senator at the time of his speech and afterward, and it was around these articles that new intensities began to gather.

Before the end of the spring term, certain students clustered around their version or versions of "The Conservative Position," and others clustered around their version or versions of "The

Liberal Position." While many of the 11,500 students remained detached, clearly a new wave of interest and activity was swelling on campus. Regular students at the University and new students transferring from other institutions launched a competitive newspaper, *The Conservative,* and members of the New Conservative Club took a major part in the controversy. The fire spread to a nearby American Legion Post, which had some key spokesmen making charges of "un-Americanism" at the University while other key spokesmen defended the university.

The Election Campaign Is Launched

During the summer, one of the two university regents up for reelection made clear that his campaign would be based on a challenge to the fitness of Mountain University's president to run the university and on the position that the university was "an autocracy" in which only liberal thought and persons had any voice in policy. "The university has fallen on evil days," the regent charged. Interwoven with the charges of "tyranny of the liberals" and "radicalism in the university" were resentments at the previous year's firing of the university's football coach and the administration's alleged lack of interest in football.

"Murderer"

Early in the fall of 1962, the campus paper printed a letter of a philosophy student, taking an extreme pacifist position. The letter referred to a number of public personalities, including Senator Goldwater. The writer made clear that he thought of anyone who considered war as a means of carrying out national policy as "a murderer." Several days after the letter appeared, a new attack struck the University with clamor that the university administration would permit a student to call a political figure of national stature a murderer. The Senator himself re-entered the controversy by his answer to the apologies of the president, of the University Board of Publications, of the editor of the paper, and of the Board of Regents, for the offending letter. The Senator's statement said the issue was one of principle, not of attacks on his person. He spoke with concern of this particular university as the only one of some 250 universities at which he had spoken, "where the socialists or whatever you care to call them seem to have the ability to do what they want without censure." He ended his reply with these words to the president: "I must because of this, then, come to the conclusion that you either do not know what's going on in the university or you don't care and in charity I will presume the former. To put it briefly, I doubt that you have the interest or the concern to be in the position you hold." This statement, coming six weeks before the local election (though not in Senator Goldwater's state) blew up a new crisis. The president's reply to Senator Goldwater made clear that "the real issue has been joined," and said the senator had made himself "a symbol of the suppressive forces which are waging an all-out assault on the University."

The president described the "genuine democracy of ideas," which the university had achieved in the face of "those who—like yourself—believe the function of a university is to indoctrinate rather than to educate, to control thought rather than to stimulate it." As for silencing those on campus who did not agree with "the American Way" as put forth in the campaign charges and in the Senator's statement, the president concluded: "Senator, I shall not silence them."

New Pressures, a Final Explosion, and the Election

Shortly after this exchange of messages, community pressures mounted to such a high point that, when a new article by the same philosophy student appeared in the campus paper, the president fired the paper's student editor, after various student-faculty-administration committees had failed to do so. New intensities and confusions swept the campus now. Some students claimed the president had in fact "silenced them." The state election followed in November, and the regent hostile to the university administration was elected by the largest vote ever recorded for a Mountain University regent. The president resigned and, in the next months, a number of key administrators left to go to new jobs elsewhere.

The dean of men and the provost had resigned some time before I arrived on campus, and the day before I arrived the dean of students announced his resignation. The president remained at his post for the remainder of the university year, and the campus and community, in the winter and spring of 1963, began to emerge from the experience with a whirl of attitudes, interpretations, questions, and convictions. It was into this setting that I arrived on campus to talk with students about their relation to "the dynamics of social and political action on college campuses."

"Our University Is Really Cliff-hanging . . ."

The newly elected president of student government, a junior, his vice-president, and two other top officers of Mountain University's student government had been eagerly describing how "things were different now" in the climate on their campus. We must have been talking together for nearly an hour before, with some cautiousness, they brought up what they called "The Subject." They had been talking about the widening interest in civil rights on campus. The student president suddenly said, "You know, this may be off your study. But it's hard to focus on James Meredith and the Freedom Rides and all the rest of it when we feel our university is really cliff-hanging. Most of the students seem unaware of what really the essence of a university is. But those who *do* care about this feel that the concept of a university which we have is really jeopardized." They began to describe the attacks on the University, and their apparent success. They spoke of the resignations of key people, the "victory for the suppressors of freedom of thought." One stressed that "the whole key is in the permissiveness of the people in these posts, in the extent they will allow freedom. They didn't fire the guy that wrote those articles about Goldwater in the campus paper. The administration put up with a lot from some of those people. We see a lot of real limitations coming after all this. We know we had it good in our freedom to speak out and act."

The student president saw the whole experience as a major

challenge to students to make student government amount to something, to have some impact on the nature of the university itself. "My real concern now is that student government here will retreat to discuss its role in lavatory maintenance and so on. It will be easy for this to happen after this past year's experience."

Why Did They Bother?

Why did these young people take on the burden of this experience this way? Why did they bother to get involved at all, and why, of all things, did they get themselves elected to top posts in the student government? I asked them this, and their answers were more revealing of what they wanted to do than of why they had sought these responsibilities. But perhaps this did answer the question. They wanted to do something for the University. The vicepresident said, "My coming into the student government was a reaction against some of the currents around here. I wanted the student government to help stabilize the University in this crisis. I thought—and think—that we can accomplish something decisive for the University." The president underscored this statement, and returned to his idea of a university. His words seemed to me then, and seem now, one of the most crucial and most heartening comments I have heard from a college student in the 1960s:

We have had here for a while an attitude toward education, toward what a university is, which I'd like to see kept and developed. It is threatened now. I saw this, and that is why I got into all this. I couldn't just stay in my classroom—actually all this seems to me very related to every minute of what goes on in my classroom. I came into this thing by the back door, to defend academic things—in the sense we have been using the word—and to defend a concept of the University. There is national threat now, from the people who want to mitigate the value of a university to society. There has to be joining of forces of students, faculty, and administration to maintain and develop the spirit of a genuine university."

No one seeing and hearing this conversation could help but be encouraged by its tone of determined hope and dedication to doing a job in and for the University. The challenge remains for students and for college administrators: how to find or develop this spirit, how to support it, nurture it, and make it work in the life of a university and beyond. It is well to remember that this young man was newly elected to his student presidency, as were his three colleagues. The real ordeals were ahead of them. But they had all had plenty of time to become cynical about the University, even about their own education. They had had ample opportunity to plunge into the minutia of organization and detail that a university of this size can provide for project-seeking students. Yet these four students had not settled for stuffiness, cynicism, or for cultivating their own academic gardens at the expense of everything else. Each had quite an extensive academic garden to cultivate, incidentally. The president was in the honors program and held the top academic award of the year before. The others were also high-powered students as well as genuinely concerned ones. They were not just bright words-and-numbers maneuverers. After some years of hearing that many of the most able students withdraw from on-and-off campus issues and responsibilities, we can be all the more impressed to see these four people in action.

Looking back on this conversation, in the light of what I was to hear later on during my visit to Mountain University and to the other campuses, I realize how very much I would like to talk to these four students today, a year later. Had the changes in administration and policy that they awaited actually taken place in the University? And, if so, how did they feel now after their year of trying "to keep student government out of lavatory maintenance and bicycle regulations"? I wonder if they did establish some kind of working relationship with faculty and administrators to maintain and develop the kind of university they were talking about.

I do not know how much contact these four people had already had with the University's administrators and key teachers. I suspect they had had little. Yet they were making the same plea I had heard from administrators about the freedom and explorative spirit of a university. If ever a partnership of some productive kind could exist between a university's student leaders and its faculty and administration, surely it would be with such students as these, who held the top positions. One could almost say it would be some kind of educational crime for a university *not* to find creative and encouragingly imaginative ways of using the intelligence and eager concern of such young people. If they and others like them were to be confined to bicycle regulations and lavatory maintenance, then I suspect there would be a great deal more lost to universities than energetic student government activities.

Close to the Storm Center

The four newly elected leaders were facing the coming year eagerly. The three outgoing leaders I encountered next were looking back to their year of leadership in shock and bitterness. They were the student ex-president and two young women who had had key roles in student government. They had been as close to the center of the university's storm as any students, sitting as they did on student-faculty-administrative committees such as the Board of Publications, before which had come some of the major crucial problems. I have no idea to what degree the administrators took these students into their confidence and how much the students just happened to observe from conveniently nearby positions. But these three ex-leaders had clearly suffered in their own ways through the whole ordeal, and it had been a shaking experience for each of them.

The ex-president was strikingly different from the new president I had met earlier. At first he seemed to be less fluent with words, less able to find abstract terms and concrete illustrations to construct a narrative or explain a position. Yet as I listened to this young man for an hour or so, I was struck by the way he found images to describe highly complex feelings and ideas. I also saw that he had less to be fluent about. He had "had it." His bitterness and disillusionment began to emerge as he moved from Castro and the Cold War to his own campus and the ugly political realities and personal futilities that had been part of his senior year education. In contrast, the newly elected student president had been challengingly, determinedly, making a case for his own hopes and plans. The former student president seemed to be trying to withdraw so that he could see what had happened, so that he could manage his own sense of shock and his own feeling that the student government role was possibly a sham, nothing more than (as he put it), "writing a check with no money in the bank." He was also studying with some caution the advantages of more detachment from the intense currents of political and personal feeling.

Who Gets Involved: The Three Groups

I was anxious to get some picture of Mountain University students as the ex-president had seen them over four years, in their response to political and social concerns and in their role in the University's campus conflict. He described a kind of satisfaction of interest and enthusiasm which echoed strongly in my mind as I thought of other campuses I had visited:

The enthusiasm goes in spurts. There is a World Affairs Conference and everyone is excited. Then that peters out and something else comes. I see three groups on the campus—maybe on any campus."

He continued to refer to these three groups in his comments during this hour, as did his two colleagues:

There is the small group that is affected continually, and they have a kind of *organic involvement* in these political and personal issues that come up. They see themselves as part of these issues. They feel related to them, they see them as moral crises, and they see their actions in the middle of them as world-shaking. The second group are people who are affected occasionally. They're the ones who respond to the spurts of interest and then forget. The third group have no relationship with all this at all.

He shifted—significantly, I thought—from "the *first* group" to "the *top* group," even though his comments seemed quietly, ruefully, to damn the naïveté and pity the agonizing of the "organically involved" students. He explained:

This top group seems to be diminishing. They feel the futility of it all. So many of them now are beginning to accept pat answers instead of going through the trauma of the struggle.

The second group, "beneath" the top, "organically involved" students, came in for a fairly close look. One of the girls commented:

This middle group sees—rightly—that there's so much to be depressed about now. Alumni tell us we should live it up, that these are the "Best Years of Our Lives." But we can't do this now. None of us can!

I asked how she saw "now" as different from five, or ten, or twenty years ago. She answered:

I think in the thirties people had spottable, physical problems. They may have been terrible, but they seemed solvable. Now the social-psychological problems are so much more complicated. You can't say as a student on this campus that you haven't enough food. You can't even say, "*there's* the enemy." The problems are so much *mistier* now than they used to be.

The ex-president added, "It ends up that the top group, the organically involved ones, just drift into the middle group. There they discuss eagerly, and forget."

Don't Let Yourself Be Affected Emotionally

Suddenly the conversation shifted into new emotional intensity, which was soon to lead into direct confrontation with the University's ordeal as these three had felt it. One girl said bitterly, "The best thing to do is not let yourself be affected emotionally. It wrecks you as a student and tears you apart." Then she added with great intensity, "A student should have *absolutely no responsibility of any kind* in the University except to learn, to grow intellectually!" She spoke with great emphasis, almost challenging the other two to contradict her. As she moved into a denunciation of the idea of student involvement in campus responsibilities outside the classroom, she made clearer and clearer how divided she was on this. She went on: "We were held responsible to aid the administration. We had to accept the responsibility and worry about all the problems, and this is just impossible." She shifted back to the idea of the nonresponsible scholar: "Except for some supercrisis in the world, a student should have *no* responsibility at all in his college years. He needs the time to form his 'self,' his values, his goals. In the future you have to have a self to fall back on. You need to achieve this self." Then, suddenly: "Now the University is falling apart, and I feel it's partly my fault. It's all how you start. They hit you with the need for people in the community to carry responsibility: 'Be a good citizen!' 'Carry your weight!' What you *ought* to do is just study."

I asked what would have been her experience at the University if she had come with the determination to remove herself from all the good-citizen-be-responsible-in-the-community pressures and "just study." She answered, "I'd have a 4.0 average by now and have had three articles published!" The ex-president ended the conversation by calling student government "an antiquated appendage." Two hours before, I had heard the newly elected student president say, "My idea of a university involves the student in a real policy-making role."

"What We Have Seen . . ."

The quieter of the girls stayed afterward and spoke about "picking up the pieces," about what some of the more "organically involved" students were feeling like doing now. "We have a lot of scars on us from all this. A lot of the kids are looking for something to do next year that has no relation to school. None of this is a question of being a liberal or a conservative, Republican, Democrat, and all that. It's the ordeal of seeing what we've seen."

What was it that she had seen? She gave an eloquent description:

It's hard to see college administrators personally suffering, to see and know their anxieties in this kind of ugly political attack. You see our college president or dean of students standing in a corner and just about yelling, "No, you've got it wrong!" and yet you see the TV and the press and the public won't listen. They just yell back, "No, we haven't got it wrong!" They talk about cleaning up a mess at the University *which we know doesn't exist*. There *is* no mess. So many of the student organizations wanted to go tell the public—you know—to get in committees and go out to the high schools and women's clubs and all that, but this was hard. We didn't know how to do it. We thought it would be too odd. We thought they might think that we were the ones indoctrinated by these "leftist radical teachers." We've seen really great professors badgered, yet we've seen them in their classes. We've seen them perform beautifully. We could tell all this, but we just didn't know how.

I wondered as I heard this, and I wonder now, about ways in which such students as this girl could have played a really helpful part in this whole storm, right in the community. Could they have gone to high schools and women's clubs to carry their side of the University's story? Could college administrators have allowed them, or encouraged them, to get that much embroiled in the controversy? Were such people as this so embroiled already that ways should have been found, on their or *someone's* initiative, to have their involvement really matter, really result in constructive action instead of frustration and bitterness?

Everybody at Mountain U. was not at nor near the storm center. Some were so far from it, or so hazy about the kind of storm it was, that it is hard to believe they shared the campus with the people whose comments have been heard here. It is in the perspective of the student responses *farther* from the storm center that the questions just raised may have special urgency. I had been talking with students who were strong in conscience, idealism, leadership ability, and concern for what a university and what an education should be. If people of such ability and dedication on campuses around the nation are only half-used, only half-involved in the major campus controversies, and if such people end up frustrated and cynical because of the ugliness of the situation and their own apparent helplessness in it, then such a political upheaval as this one is not only a tragedy for outstanding young leaders, but it is also a generally devastating experience for a university.

If even a handful of students are ready to serve, help, understand a situation, and speak out on it, but a way is not worked out to let them do so, then the subject of what a university can do to encourage thinking and sensitivity in its apathetic, confused, or generally preoccupied students is hardly worth bothering about.

Farther from the Storm Center

Not everybody on Mountain University's campus felt as close to the storm center as, say, the retiring student president. Some "Greeks" seemed to have a vague sense of "something messy" going on, but their main response to the whole explosion had to do with the "value," as they put it, of the diploma of Mountain University and what might be happening to it. Some students had remote and garbled versions of the facts and emotions that had led to the resignation of their president and several key administrators. And some, already tired of all the talk and publicity, all the rallies and arguments, had turned back to their own studies, their own special interests, or, in the case of some politically and socially concerned groups, to their new efforts on the local and national scene.

A major theme with these students was that "people"—of the state and beyond—must be getting a queer idea of Mountain University "from all this publicity and racket." A young sophomore student government representative spoke with real worry: "There is such a fear going around the community and the state, a fear of Communist influence on campus. There is a sort of image of the campus as a huge collection of beards and sandals and radical opinions."

The farther I got from the student leaders, the more concern I heard about "those elements" in the student body who were causing trouble. The beards and sandals seemed easy labels for them. Yet I heard attacks on student leaders for their participation in the whole controversy, even though the leaders were as far as could be imagined from the beatnik elements that seemed to trouble the students with whom I was talking.

A number felt that the university's really exciting days were suddenly at an end, with suspicion and caution and repression looming over the horizon. Some spoke of the "real fire" in the paper, in classes, in conversations, which was going out. I saw and heard strong emotion in connection with this idea, as in the case of the girl who cried, "The people of this state can't bear to have this university *be* a university." Another said that the adventure and discovery in her education at M.U. was on the way out, and a perfect symbol of this was "yesterday's nice little article in the *Conservative* about 'leftist tendencies' in our best physics man. That is really the end!"

Just Something Political

As I moved farther from the center of the controversy, I was more and more struck by the vagueness of students' understanding of the furor. An evening at one of the fraternities pointed up this vagueness, this sense that there was a problem, but that its outline was so indistinct that it was easier to think about suspicious individuals or pat slogans to "explain" it all.

After what I had heard from some of the student government people, the sense of involvement with the University's conflict, the feeling of "being partly responsible for the University's falling apart," the new student president's feeling of the University being threatened by people trying to coerce thought on campus—after all this, I was startled to hear it dealt with at a fraternity by just one sentence: "It is just something political." Another student added: "The political problems are not really significant to what goes on on this campus."

Only two of the students were in-state residents. But does this by itself account for the detachment of these fraternity men from an ordeal that had cost the University its president and several other top people all within a year? I could only infer that "something political" satisfied them because it implied something both irrelevant to their real interests and something murky, an area of doubt and wrangling and complexity—and probably corruption—that it was as well not to dig into it. The one prober in the room said: "You all admit there is some freedom and excitement there that is worth something. These things are going out now. Think of how the University has been built up in the past few years." Most seemed to agree automatically that the University *had* made great strides in the last few years, particularly in terms of "moving away from the party school image." One man asked: "Did all this upbuilding come with the college president?"

Some insisted that it had. "Yet here we are," one said pessimistically, "with people saying the University is radical and full of oddballs and going to pot. Our degree will look bad with all these wild charges."

An Evening at a Sorority

"There are some of our brightest, finest juniors and seniors in that sorority." One of the deans had told me this before I visited one of the sororities for dinner. I met with particular friendliness and interest. About fifteen young women launched eagerly into the University's experience of the past year, and continued for nearly two hours. The emphasis fell quickly on "the deteriorating image" of the University resulting from attacks of wild-eyed radicalism. They seemed to see the issue itself pretty much in some kind of aura around the president's acts, his personality, his presence, or his absence: "We have always heard that there's something wrong with M.U.'s president."

Where the fraternity men had tried to push aside the whole subject, these young women wanted to discuss it purely in terms of a college president's style, or what other people said about his style. They seemed to have as little information on the actual facts as the men had. They dealt with the murkiness of it all by saying, "You can't find the truth out about these things anyway."

The Classroom as an Island

How much do or should major campus issues, especially those with national reverberations, be injected into the life of actual college courses? With accusations flying and factions deploying, professors might understandably want to avoid accepting some commitment themselves, preferring to keep the subject closed. Others might feel that the issue was overdiscussed and that class time should not be used for more rehashing. Now that the fence-sitting professor is under heavy attack from student groups around the country, the question of campus controversy in the classroom is raging. Students who were furious at the idea of being propagandized in class were often the first to complain of a professor who did not take a stand and say where he stood.

To what extent should the faculty in a campus situation similar to that of Mountain University involve themselves and their students in any kind of factual exploration of events, let alone any philosophical exploration of what it all means? I wondered about the faculty's possible contribution to sense and awareness more removed from the firing line than the key administrators. With a different kind of access to students, the faculty could be useful in helping students to some kind of understanding and examination of the issues. But I saw little of this from the students at M.U.

What If . . . ?

I asked the sorority what would have happened if one of the deans or professors had visited each fraternity, sorority, and dormitory to attempt to describe the situation as seen by key people in the University when these explosions were happening. The first answers were eagerly enthusiastic. All agreed that the students would have welcomed this. Then reservations appeared: "Wouldn't administrators and key teachers have had to hedge and cover up, use double-talk?" Others thought that this might well have happened. No one suggested any special reason for hedging and double-talk. They assumed some kind of mystery that was too deep for anybody in power to discuss frankly with students. Yet I saw no hint of anyone in the room accepting the charges of "liberal brainwashing of students," "liberal autocracy," "administrative inefficiency," and the rest.

Any Way Out?

Is there any way that students like these young women could be brought into the confidence of a university administration or of a faculty about a major on-and-off campus political issue? Would such an effort have to drown in "hedging and double-talk"? Would administrative frankness, and a real effort to enlist students in some kind of understanding of the issue have to be interpreted as more "liberal brainwashing"? Would this eventually make more or fewer problems on a campus?

An issue like this needs to be faced, examined, and understood as a crucial part of a student's education. One hears much about "relevance" and its importance in reaching students and challenging them to think about their education and their world. Mountain U.'s ordeal was a perfect case history of a campus explosion that would seem to be relevant to the students, to their view of their campus and their nation. Students involved in even a portion of the deliberations, discussions, and decisions cared passionately. But beyond this limited involvement, why could there not be a facing of the issues, promoted and carried out by administrators, professors, and concerned students?

Some assumptions are too easy for an observer to accept. One is that the students would not care to be informed or enlisted in the issue in such a direct way. Faculty and administrators' explanations and interpretations might have made students suspicious, wary of being indoctrinated, hostile to a discussion of anything that sounded as if an opinion were buried in it. That kind of response is possible. But might not students welcome a direct encounter with student leaders and key adults on campus as to what the events of the ordeal "meant"? This could dispel charges of indoctrination in one interpretation. Admittedly, most of the administrators at the top would have held a similar interpretation of what was happening. Faculty members did not, however, and there was opportunity for students, as an actual educational experience, to explore facts and interpretations in search of their own understanding.

If some kind of conversation between administrators, professors, and students had been launched in an organized way, new problems might have arisen in off-campus efforts to tell a story. Yet the off-campus intensities were already on-campus, in the *Conservative* and expressed by some of its newly arrived staff. If community leaders of various views had scrambled for students' support of this or that view, would this necessarily have been unhealthy as a part of the students' education to some psychological and political realities?

Theoretical answers to these questions would be different from those for a specific campus in the midst of an actual ordeal. But in the often-discussed matter of student apathy, one gets the feeling that apathy is an unmovable, uniform body. The confusion, misinformation, and the superficial semiexplanations in which so many students floundered as they discussed the University's ordeal, did not have the character of apathy. But the refusal to try to sort out opinion and fact from study of the regular liberal newspaper and of the newly established conservative newspaper on campus *was* a form of apathy.

I suppose different people treat an explosion in their environment in different ways. Perhaps student governments as well as university professors and administrators have to wrestle with the implications of this simple tendency. Otherwise, a campus may easily remain divided among the automatically dedicated few—those who can see an issue in terms of their own particular battle-cries—and "The Rest," who are classified as "apathetic." A big question mark stands over "The Rest," over the possibility for their eventual concern and understanding of the issues, given a chance to care about and to understand the actualities, and granting their potential for constructive action as undergraduates, as alumni and as citizens.

5

Civil Rights

It is no longer news that there are college students around the country who are passionately concerned and personally identified with the struggle of American Negroes for many different and significant kinds of equality in our society. The term Civil Rights has come to mean that struggle almost exclusively. In this study, it was fascinating to see the varieties of this interest, from intense and personal involvement, to uncomfortable negativism, to a kind of assenting remoteness. Fascinating, too, were the differences among students and among campuses in the ways students *act* on these feelings, ways they found to take part in the whole movement (if they did take part), and ways they found to express their sense of identification with it, their sense of being concerned watchers, detached discussers, suspicious viewers, or simply busy students.

One university had students in jails in Mississippi and Alabama. I wondered what they would think of the stage of awareness and concern in the university I visited, which was busy collecting thousands of books to send to a southern Negro college. While one university was raising money to send students to the South to help with Negro voter registration, another was sending a small YMCA group to towns in Texas, Arkansas, and Mississippi to observe, study, and talk with other college students, all committed to keep clear of any agitation. Still another campus was so embroiled in the local and national reverberations of a political attack on the university that the Negro's struggle came up only in one highly intelligent but quite abstract three-hour discussion among twenty-five students talking about the peace movement.

What follows here is not, of course, an analysis of the extent or intensity of each campus's concern and action in the matter of the Negro's struggle for equality. It is a series of contrasting conversations and observations with people whom I met, chosen because they had a particular interest in the subject or had brought up the subject while we were talking about something else. Out of these conversations comes, obviously, no "Civil Rights quotient" or ratio of concern to action that is demonstrable by graph or Geiger counter. The conversations *do* show individual students with special feelings of concern or lack of them. They show something of the influence of such students on each other. They show something about how students and administrators can see and hear each other, or fail to do so. And they show something of the enormous range of perceptions about the subject, from indifference on through degrees of awareness and identification to a whole-hearted plunging into the spirit of revolution itself, at the actual barricades, with the college campus left far behind.

City U. and the Freedom Riders' Loan

City University's uproar over a loan to some students who had gone on a summer Freedom Ride may sound remote to those deafened by current headlines about campus explosions. But it was a significant moment in the life of City U., and brought new and healthy concerns to the fore. It made student government move into a new role, which key administrators and key students agreed was more purposeful and dignified than it had been before. Not the least of the results of this experience was the communication discovered or established between students and deans, even at the most emotional moments of the controversy.

Nine of City U.'s 26,000 students had gone by bus to Mississippi in the summer of 1963. Before they went, some deans and advisors had tried to dissuade them. They spoke of the danger of their being hurt and the real possibility that these students could be more effective in other ways. Five of the nine students were

Negroes, and I gather these five were among the most concerned and most intellectually able Negroes on the campus. It was agreed (or at least words to this effect were exchanged) that the ride was an individual matter, and that there was a state law that the name of the University could not be given to support any social or political movement. The students on the ride had been promised financial support and aid for possible bail and other expenses by CORE. When they got to Jackson they were arrested. Some of the bail money did come from CORE, but instead of having the bail simply paid and the matter dropped, there was a series of legal problems involving repeated appeals and a long struggle in the courts. Eight of the students returned to City U. in the fall. Two had been killed in an airplane crash. (Their trip was not a part of their summer's effort as Freedom Riders or of their work in Mississippi.) The eight students reported to the dean and told their story. The legal expenses were getting very high, and CORE could not provide all the funds. They raised the question of how the University might help raise these funds. The University administration suggested, through the dean, some possibilities, including a system of personal loans or an off-campus fund-raising program with publicity on the campus.

The conversation about this went on for about three months. Then some of the students struck on the idea of asking for a loan to the *group*, rather than to individuals, the money to come from the student council. The student council said its funds, earmarked for campus activities, should not have to cover this kind of project. The students involved then went to the University's Board of Control, asking if this Board could make the loan to the group. There followed petitions for a student referendum on whether the Board of Control, which is responsible to the chancellor of the University, should lend this money to the group or whether it should not. The students voted in favor of such a loan. The problem was that the funds of the Board of Control are compulsorily collected from students, and other of its funds come from profits from student activities. There is also a law that the University cannot be committed to social or political causes. The Board of Control decided against the loan. The students launched a mass-protest meeting, followed by an appeal to the chancellor, who was out of town. The vice-chancellor upheld the Board of Control's refusal to make the loan. The student leaders went directly to the chancellor when he returned, and the chancellor upheld the refusal.

There was some well-organized picketing in which the students behaved responsibly. The picketing went on with the dean's protection and consent, with coffee served and police in attendance to see that the picketers were not interfered with.

The resolution of the whole matter came when a student loan fund granted loans to *individuals*. This had been the original suggestion made by the administration, but at the beginning there had been some argument and confusion as to whether each of the eight students was eligible for a loan. (Some had been granted other loans earlier.) The administrators said it was always clear that this problem could be solved, but some of the students claimed they did not understand this. At any rate the money was raised for the eight students as individuals.

Versions and Reverberations

What I read and heard about this actual series of events seemed less significant than the quality of interest and concern that it produced and the kind of student-administration communication and understanding that developed for some people, if not for others. One of the deans said:

This whole business was well worthwhile, it seems to me. It took the student interests and concerns on this campus out of the apathetic doldrum of student government. All this aroused the students. It began a viable exchange of student thought. It also brought "the southern problem" home to everybody here in a new way and started a new awareness. Also—and I think this is important—I really believe it didn't leave any personal animosity. Instead, it triggered a preoccupation of student government with larger issues than the ones they had been dealing with. It set up, I would say, a whole new trend of consequential thinking.

Facts and emotions, misconceptions and resentments were still whirling around the campus. One of the Freedom Riders told me, "The real issue was that the students have the right to have a say in the spending of student funds." Another one of the riders said, "The university sees student activity as something to keep under constraint. They say, 'How do we keep this at a minimum?' " One of the students on the campus newspaper told me, "Those people needed money and there was a big controversy, but it was not a liberal-conservative conflict and it wasn't an administration-student conflict either. Actually there were students on the Board of Control." Other students certainly didn't agree with this view. I talked to some students who said with conviction that they felt their main aim was to "make things hard for the liberals around here." They had had a booth on the campus during the loan controversy. They kept a student in it all day and on into the evening, getting petitions *against* the Freedom Riders' loan. Other students had booths and workers getting petitions *for* the loan. One girl spoke to me about seeing a fraternity man sitting in his booth calling out for signatures against the loan: "I just went up to him and took him by the collar and *shook* him! Yet all I could think of to say was, 'How can you *do* this, how can you *do* this?' "

Obviously all 26,000 of City University's students were not in an uproar about this loan, even at the height of the excitement, let alone several months later. And there were perhaps inevitable scars and some brooding among some of the students most involved. A remarkable feature of this aftermath was that, all through my conversations, I had the impression that the personnel deans and advisors were in continual communication with the various elements of the student body most concerned: the Freedom Riders themselves, the strongest advocates of the loan, and the strongest opponents of it. This in itself is a significant achievement, even though the administrators had to bear a good many accusations of restrictiveness, stuffiness, coerciveness. The evidences of good communication and even good will between students and personnel people would have been impressive in a campus of 500, let alone one of 26,000.

Aftermath

The issues and interests at City U. had clearly changed in only a few months. Those most active, most devoted to the student-riders loan issue were now tackling new problems, with special interest in the ban on Communist speakers (shortly afterward lifted in the state). I met with students in most of the discussion groups, and there was no all-out driving interest in Civil Rights as *the* issue, as there had been before. Some of the students wanted simply to talk about the other campus liberal organizations and their in-fighting. Several students seemed to deplore this especially. As one student said about the other students who were supposedly active and concerned in Civil Rights, "Too many of them won't *stick* to anything. A few of us do stick to our concerns. We care about them. A lot of the rest feel it's all a waste of time unless there's some big, grand, dramatic explosion about something."

Whether or not that fellow was fair in his judgment, the question remains as to what students should *do* and still remain in college? I kept meeting students at City University and on some of the other campuses who spoke of a roommate who had gone to Birmingham, an older brother now working for the NAACP, a last year's student officer now working with a Negro voter registration unit in Mississippi. For those still on campus, it had to be the business meeting, the plans for picketing or talk about the futility of picketing, the sudden response to headlines and the plans for a rented bus for Jackson, the dissipation of the enthusiasm and the hope for some kind of release of feelings into action. All these things had to suffice until there could be a real focus of intensity like that of the Freedom Riders' loan issue at City U.

Contrasts Elsewhere

Of the campuses I visited, only at City U. had there been a major Civil Rights issue around which masses of students could rally and demonstrate. On the other campuses, Civil Rights as a subject was something that was discussed wherever students gathered to discuss anything beyond personal and campus matters.

Students flocked to hear and question speakers who had extreme positions on Civil Rights, such as Governor Wallace and Malcolm X. CORE groups were developing on some campuses, though often the main thrust of interest and effort in Civil Rights did not originate in the CORE group on campus or in the community. Fields University was in the midst of a "Civil Rights drive" to raise $5,000 to help send college students from around the nation to Mississippi for programs in literacy and history, aimed at vastly increasing voter registration. A few students emphasized to me that this was CORE's achievement. Others said this was the achievement of the U.S. National Student Association and the university's student president of the previous year.

At any rate, the Civil Rights drive seemed to be a generally accepted and approved project, an all-campus interest. I talked to some students who were fairly uninterested in it, or who disapproved of it, but there was no sense of a fight for or against the drive. There was no administration versus student issue about it, no liberal versus conservative fight carried on in the open. The student government (see Chapter 7) of Fields University had inherited a concern from the preceding year's leaders and was acting on it with the cooperation of the student newspaper and, I gathered, of most of the students who were at all actively interested in the world beyond the campus. One newspaper editor disposed of the CORE group on campus with this statement: "Its followers are people that nobody knows. They are grad students—very level headed, determined, all out for one cause." Yet others admitted that CORE had brought some life to campus discussions of Civil Rights. They lined up an impressive minister to "answer" Governor Wallace in an adjoining hall, right after Wallace's speech to the students. This was evidently one of the liveliest evenings on the Fields campus in some time. But, again, the concern with Civil Rights was general, not the possession of any one group or commitment at Fields. There was an evident disownment of the "hot headed characters with their radical ideas," as one girl described them. Yet she was wholeheartedly in support of the student government's Civil Rights drive for that $5,000. She explained, "I'm all for it. And I don't need to join some group to find people who agree with me. I think maybe a lot of us have the feeling that we've had our fill of radicals this year and that we want to 'go steady' for a while. But that doesn't mean we are giving up our ideals!"

Civil Rights and the College Student

There has been a good deal of tempting and satisfying generalization about college students' (or, even more satisfying, *the* college student's) response to the national Civil Rights crisis. The generalizations tend to fall away when one visits a campus, almost any campus, since the range of attitudes on Civil Rights remains so wide. Still, there is no question that for some of the students I have encountered (only a small number were Negroes), the Civil Rights drama in our country has seized their imaginations and their consciences in powerful ways. The identification with the struggle of Negroes for rights and opportunities is so intense, in some students, that their feelings are not simply opinions or attitudes toward a problem. They become a part of these young people's emotional and intellectual landscape, inseparable from what they think of as their own selves. The students I met who feel this way have a hard time even taking seriously another national problem, sometimes even another personal problem. These people are on the Freedom Rides, on the picket lines, in the active campus drives, or they have left college temporarily or permanently to work full time for the cause.

This relatively small number seems to have a surprising influence on the attitudes, and sometimes the consciences, of less concerned students. I found pockets of real hostility to any talk about Civil Rights or to campus activities committing a college to some position about Civil Rights. But I saw very little *apathy* about Civil Rights as a national issue. This may well have resulted from the influence of the personally engaged students I have just been describing. I suspect it may also result from national climate, in and out of the mass media, in which Civil Rights is so crucial a matter. There may be a relatively small handful that seizes the opportunity to go, to serve, to make noise, to explode ideas and feelings and desires on the campus and beyond it. But many of "the others" listen and share at least periods of concern and excitement. They support the dedicated ones when the crisis comes. They talk earnestly about Civil Rights, give money to a cause, sometimes give time and thoughtfulness before turning back to the textbook, or the laboratory, or the party.

Even the most ill-informed students I met, at least in the area of Civil Rights, would stress that "our compassion for the Negro is as good as *theirs*." "Theirs" would almost always refer either to the most respected and dedicated students or to the most noisy and activist ones, not necessarily the same people.

For some students it may be that the Civil Rights crisis offers an emotional free ride. But this is shaky ground for generalizing and interpreting. It is easy to label one student as sincerely dedicated and another as emotionally joy-riding. A twenty-year-old may sound, as he talks about a Civil Rights explosion somewhere in the country, as if he were talking about his own *personal* struggle for equality, for recognition, for fair treatment from "them," the adults. Thus, some white students see themselves as "like" the Negroes, and the adult world corresponds in their feelings to "the white world" in the view of the Negroes with whom they feel such kinship. The intense feelings of these twenty-year-olds' for "freedom" may come from personal struggles and desires, which somehow substitute the Negroes' struggle for a somewhat different meaning of "freedom," and thus identification with a cause is made. The danger lies in saying too easily that this identification is "just" a late-adolescent feeling of antiadult struggle or personal identity struggle, hooked onto a convenient national issue. This would be a worse mistake than to say rather naïvely that this identification represents a new sensitivity of conscience and commitment to service on the part of *the* college student.

I would be slow to dismiss the significance, even the sincerity, of the emotional free rider on the Civil Rights bandwagon. Sometimes these students are nuisances on a campus, embarrassing other students and irritating deans. And still others may seem to be cold-bloodedly using Civil Rights issues to make themselves important, or influential, or at least heard. But the motives are complicated enough to deserve better appraisal from spectators and commentators. Easy labels that classify who is sincere and who is a troublemaking gamesman, who is really dedicated and who is having an emotional ride, who is serving a cause and who is serving himself, are poor alternatives. The Civil Rights issue has seized college students in extraordinarily complicated ways, and has produced some remarkably varied behavior. The main point is that it *has* seized so many of them. It is apart from the vestiges of apathy. It is in the air students breathe.

The *styles* of students' responses, as I saw them in my visits, may range from the young man returning from an Alabama jail with a broken back, waiting to recover sufficiently to go back again and help with voter registration, to the girl quietly tutoring the eleven-year-old Negro child from a neighboring slum; from the sophomore dropout working full time for the NAACP, to the fraternity man who says he cares about Civil Rights but "just doesn't go for all this telegram and petition stuff"; from the philosophical talker who links Civil Rights and the peace movement and liberal causes as part of his world's most interesting challenges, to the fellow who left eight hours' work in the library to stand uncomfortably and dazed in the jammed hall where Governor Barnett was speaking, listening intently during speech and questioning, and then returning to the library in silence.

The campus explosions about Civil Rights may come at the times of year when student explosions always come—exam time, just before spring, and other usual periods of tension. But they come at other times, too, and their nature is quite different from the old panty raids and even the "new" campus riots. "Concern" in some degree is the watchword, to the point where deans are talking about "concern" and students accuse each other of failure to have concern or of "going overboard" with concern. For most, the Civil Rights concern is not steady. Other intensities rush in frequently and crowd it out. But it is there as a part of the landscape, inner and outer, of many college students, and it smolders in ways that do indeed make "a new ferment on the campus."

6

Politics:
Voices from Right, Left,
and Off-Center

Politics was a lively and explosive interest on some (not all) of the campuses I visited. I saw little of the timidity about expressing political enthusiasm that one heard so much about on campuses of the fifties. There remain plenty of students who are totally immersed in their books, labs, and partying. Everyone is not so "politically awakened" as some of the more optimisitc and eulogistic commentators are proclaiming. Nevertheless, many of the self-proclaimed apolitical students emerge from their study stalls, their fraternities, and their city apartments when a newsworthy speaker drops onto the campus to speak. As one student said, "if there's some headline controversy about him, they'll flock in to hear him or, more likely, to get a look at him."

The bursting auditorium suggests "everyone's" passionate interest, but a look at a total campus may not. A university's largest hall may overflow with students who want to see and hear Senator Goldwater, Dean Rusk, or Governor Wallace. Yet there may be four, or five, or six times as many students who are *not* in that hall and are busy doing something else. At City University, a "huge turnout" to hear the head of the economics department debate a local John Birch Society official actually meant a turnout of 800 of the university's 26,000 students. The number of students excited by the most sensational political figures or issues of the day may be larger than it was a decade ago, but what is the quality of this interest? Who has it? How do they express it? How does it affect their lives and the life of the campus itself? How does it reach beyond the campus? What does it mean for the student's life after graduation?

No single study is going to answer these questions satisfactorily. This one can best show something of the *quality* of interest—of fraternity-sorority conversations about community attacks on the campus, of Young Socialist and Young Conservatives struggling to make clear their position to each other and to a visitor, of student government leaders agitating for this or that speaker to visit the campus, of the support of the so-called seriously dedicated and the so-called wild-eyed irresponsibles for this or that political effort.

The Philosophical Conservatives

In the past few years there has been a great deal written about a "wave of political conservatism" among college students. I saw little evidence of it on the campuses I visited. The only *organized* interest in political conservatism was at Mountain University, where the administration had been under a year-long attack for its alleged "liberal brainwashing" and discrimination against conservative positions and those holding them. A lively and dedicated Conservative Club and an attractive and highly polished newspaper, *The Conservative*, were attempting to challenge the regular campus paper and its alleged "automatic liberalism." The *Conservative* was wholeheartedly in sympathy with the attacks on the University administration and certain teachers and students. Its editor was clearly the leader of the conservative position among the students already committed to it. He had come onto the campus the summer before, from a succession of other universities where he had been a graduate student. He would challenge visiting dignitaries to debate, stand up in meetings to give the expected conservative rebuttal, rally and encourage discussion and argument for the conservative side, and write vigorous statements for his cause in the papers.

A good many students at M.U. were awed by the eloquence and energy of this new arrival on campus, whether or not they agreed with him. His supporters referred to him with the greatest respect, considering him a more-than convenient asset to their cause on this campus at this time.

None of the conservatives made reference to the recent arrival or the campus-hopping background of their editor-leader, though less sympathetic students had a lot to say about this. I was struck with how eager these young men were to "keep the political discussion on a philosophical plane." None I met were especially militant or wild-eyed, but they were highly verbal and very serious about what they kept calling "our philosophy." They were eager to make a dent in the University's thinking about "the libel against Goldwater" and "the liberal control of thinking." They would quote a lawyer-father, or Ayn Rand, or William Buckley, or Senator Goldwater to pinpoint their grievances against the University administration and those on its side. Sometimes the tone was conspiratorial: "We can see that the administration doesn't like us and we don't like them." They saw an attempt to control them, especially by means of an effort to get the names of the financial backers for the obviously expensive newspaper. The Conservative Club's president felt a strong responsibility to the *Conservative's* financial backers and to their anonymity. This was a key issue. "The University wants to check our finances—find out who the donors are. We got $30,000 coming in and these backers need assurance that the money will be spent according to their philosophy. This is a private organization just like U.S. Steel or any other. Only state courts can get us to give out financial sources." He suddenly reversed his field: "Yet the university accuses us of being controlled by our contributors! We are not. That's irrelevant anyway. We should be judged by what we say, not by who finances us."

Philosophical, Not Political

The handful of conservative students I encountered at Mountain U. spoke with defensive, sometimes hostile words, but with a

tone that was cordial and agreeable and which sounded reason-
able. They were eager for "more talk, more activation of the
minds around here." Their main aim was, as one said, "to challenge the basic moods prevalent at this University." They saw
themselves as "a philosophical organization inspired by philosophers like Ayn Rand and others, a philosophy about man's relation to his government and his society." The Club president spoke
firmly on this: "If a politician attaches himself to this philosophy,
that's fine, but we are interested in the philosophical side."

Philosophical or not, much of the activity in the group was
devoted to specific events, people, and issues on campus: Who
could sue whom for the "libel" in the regular campus paper, attacks on the University's Board of Publications, "which," one
young man said, "is trying to suppress us." But along with their
immersion in the campus ordeal, there was an on-going effort to
influence students, particularly freshmen. "We never hoped to
dent seniors," the Club president said. "We hoped to get some
juniors and sophomores in a bind, and to get them to question
things they've been taught. But the real hope is the freshmen. The
discussion gets violent sometimes, but people come back the next
night for more, and that's encouraging."

One of the fascinating themes in these conversations was the
disenchantment with fraternities and sororities. Supposedly the
stronghold of conservatism of many sorts, the fraternities and
sororities were incompatible with some of the strong-minded conservatives who talked about them. Their reason was not that the
fraternity-sorority students were too far to the "left." It was that
the Greek houses didn't care about philosophical-political things
enough, from any point of view. Thus I would come from a talk
with a vociferous liberal who was discouraged by the "apathy and
conservatism" in the Greek houses to a talk with a vociferous
conservative who lamented the fraternity student's preoccupation
with "cars and girls and money and clothes and drinking." I heard
some reference among conservatives of the right of a fraternity to
discriminate "if it wants to." (I did not hear this from inside a
fraternity or sorority, however.) One conservative student re-
gretted that the fraternities did not seize this right and make a

genuine intellectual issue of it. It was a sad, lost opportunity: "The fraternities are not providing an atmosphere for intellectual challenge. They represent the basic concept of private property. They have a wonderful chance and yet they don't seize it—they're just juveniles."

Wherever I heard the conservative position on this campus, it was with great stress on the new, revolutionary spirit of conservatism. These students felt they had hold of something so dynamic and exciting that all they needed was to open up discussions, launch debates, challenge other students to think for themselves, and that then the students would catch fire in this new spirit. Yet intertwined with the enthusiasm would be bitter comments about the forces rallied against them and doctrinaire, sometimes baffling "of-course" remarks on the current scene such as, "You can have peace via totalitarian power, which the U.N. could so easily become if it got to be a big enough bully and got a big enough club. That's force—the U.N.'s philosophy of force. You can't have force. We're opposed to force and the U.N.'s whole principle is force."

Aftermath

Within several months, the *Conservative* had disbanded on campus and its visiting grad-student editor had gone elsewhere. Those supporting the paper may have felt that their main goal, the removal of the University's top administrators, had been achieved. Since the anti-university-and-administration trustees had been overwhelmingly elected, and since the University's president and several key administrators had subsequently resigned, the outside "antiliberal establishment" forces that had reached onto this particular campus simply went elsewhere.

But what of the enthusiastic conservatives who remained to complete their undergraduate requirements? Theirs was clearly not a temporary interest. Their insistence on "staying on a philosophical plane," suggested a position and an effort that was far from fleeting. For a time they had the support of money and energetic people from outside. These had withdrawn now that the major battles had been won against the alleged "liberal brain-washers" on the campus administration, particularly the president who had resigned. Nevertheless, the remaining students who had been caught up in this effort were not about to drop their sense of excitement just because of their small number and a change for the better, in their view, in the campus climate.

The Antiliberals

If Mountain U. was the only campus where I found any organized and vigorous effort for political conservatism even among a small group of dedicated students, City U. provided some unusually articulate and determined students who, if unorganized, were earnest spokesmen for what they called "antiliberalism." This was a very different spirit from that of the conservative philosophers at M.U. This was nonintellectual in tone, without any of the sense of excitement or "new philosophical wave" that had so buoyed the spirit of the M.U. conservative group. Those students I met who considered themselves conservatives, even actual leaders of conservative opinion, were not part of any campus organization. One said he belonged to the Young Republicans, but was "very disenchanted with the group president's being a liberal Republican." He was considering splitting away from the YR's and starting a group of Young Americans for Freedom at City U. He spoke appreciatively of this group as "a right-wing counterpart of the Young Socialist Alliance—Bill Buckley and Fulton Lewis III are among the sponsors." Yet he and others in this small group, which I can only call negative conservatives, saw themselves as "the oddities around here." They saw City U's climate as predominantly liberal and themselves as holdouts against the faculty's liberalizing efforts.

Among these people there seemed to be real resentment for the liberals' confident entrenchment at City U. "They think they are right and that everybody agrees with them. Well, everybody doesn't." It became clearer and clearer that the people holding this view saw themselves simply as patient builders of road blocks in the way of the liberal traffic. "We shocked them," one said, "when we came out against NAACP and CORE and the Young Democrats." Others spoke of their hostile views toward the campus newspaper, though they pointed to few efforts to do anything about these views. The main effort had been against the Freedom Riders' loan. "We fought for two weeks. We typed up petitions. Four of us ran the whole delaying operation—we set up a booth on campus and we got 1,400 signatures against the loan. *They* had 4,000. This was our biggest success. And there were tremendous forces lined up against us."

Time Out for Apathy

These negative conservatives had in common with the enthusiasts of the other side on their campus a dark view of apathy on their campus. "People on this campus just don't care at all." The liberal students were as likely to shift from talking about the conservatives and their wrong headedness to the subject of campus apathy. The conservatives had a more sinister view of the opposition, the active and self-confident liberals. The conservatives were furiously resistant; they attacked not only the leftists and the apathetic, but the "wrong-headed" Young Republicans. One man said that the head of one faction of the Young Republicans was also head of a student American Civil Liberties Union group. "Now how can you possibly understand *that?*"

NSA—The Real Enemy

Most of the conservatives I talked with gave the impression of having the goods on their opponents. Now they would see them as threatening; now they would see them as comic. Yet, to them, the serious problem was the general assumption of "so-called liberal answers and attitudes as the only ones" on campus. The strongest force perpetuating this atmosphere seemed, in their minds, to be the U.S. National Student Association. One student said, "There are no issues on campus for us to coalesce around," and the man with him said grimly, "There's one issue—my idea would be to get the N.S.A. kicked off campus. That would really rally our kind of people."

One young man, who had had the most vitriolic comments about the sinister elements among his campus' student groups, said, "What we really need is a constructive issue. People think we're negative all the time. The trouble is that *they* have the advantage in terminology. I mean, they say we're anti-Freedom Riders' loan. It sounds as if we were antifreedom. They shouldn't call it the freedom riders' loan. The robbery loan would be better. They say we're pro–un-American Activities Committee. As if we were pro–un-American activities! We're the conservatives trying to upset the status quo. We're actually the radicals!"

It Used to Be Called Liberalism

Whenever politics was discussed, there were many meanings of the word "liberal" hanging over the conversation. The conservatives spoke of "the liberals" with some contempt. But the main stream of opinion and concern, which one would easily be called *liberalism*, seems to move ahead without much reference to the name. A good deal of this hesitancy has to do with attitudes in some of the state legislatures toward the colleges and universities. Students spoke of repeated attacks on the "liberalism" of their campus, launched from the floor of their state legislatures and echoed at home dinner tables and at vacation times. The word *"liberal"* has so often been used as though it meant questionable things, so that students simply gave it up and described specific interests and attitudes instead. One of the staff of a campus newspaper spoke of himself as "a Democrat but not particularly a liberal."

It may be that students who care about the cluster of causes and attitudes and feelings that were once gathered under the term *liberalism* now tend to be more specific and discriminating in how they talk about their concerns, and are less satisfied with such a large as well as battered general term as "liberalism."

Echoes from the McCarthy era rang with some force on some campuses. Campus newspaper staffs were most likely to evoke these echoes. A favorite topic was the swing to and from politically conservative editors. One newspaper staff writer said, "There is still some hangover from the McCarthy days, and there are some new doings that are causing trouble. There are kids who are pretty wary about their letters to the editor, or even about doing controversial research papers. And you hear a lot of this little red schoolhouse and Moscow University business." One young man laughed and said, "You know, my parents were here thirty years ago and they heard the same thing, from the legislature and from their home town. Yet this is supposed to be one of the great universities in the country. You'd think the people of the state were scared to death of the University!" I heard my own set of echoes as he spoke: of the students at beleagered Mountain U. who had spoken of preserving the *idea* of a university, and of the boy who had spoken in desperation of the congressman who said that his university had no business teaching Chinese and Russian, since the state was landlocked.

Centers of Intense Interest

Where I found lively interest in political things was in the concerns and attitudes of what was once easily called "liberalism." Those on the liberal side, whatever labels they used or however they managed to avoid labels, showed little of the defensiveness of their counterparts on the right. This group of campuses had very few students who stood toward the extreme left. I did talk with a few avowed socialists, though even these were not clustered together in any way that seemed to satisfy them as being an organization. They were simply students with a position—almost, on one campus, community freaks. (The president of a student socialist group told me rather plaintively, "I stand on the walk and give out leaflets and now, since the time I was beaten up, there are usually some other students who are around to see that it doesn't happen again. They don't go along with my beliefs but they didn't like my getting beaten up, so they stand up for me!") On another campus, the socialist group reflected a good deal more energy than did this young president, but the energy went into antics and demonstrations in which the participants seemed to have little faith, or into earnest and vigorous participation in the campus liberal causes, in which they were clearly in the minority. These

included peace movements, Civil Rights activities, and active interest in questioning visitors who espoused either left or right
views.

But vigorous interest in politics, when there was interest at all,
was in the liberal tradition, usually with a new vocabulary and a
search for new ways of effective action beyond mere talk. Thus,
students interested in the peace movement would find that a lot of
the talk in the Student Peace Union meeting would be about in-
tegration or local politics. Students meeting to discuss a Civil
Rights march would get onto the Cold War and the arms race.
Some found this unfocused and irritating. It may be a strength,
however, that many students see the *relatedness* of some of the
issues that are knotted so tightly in our society and our world.

A Sense of Urgency

These impressions, it should be remembered, are based on conversations with the people who cared. On some campuses, these
were harder to find than on others. And the caring related to what
the students considered "politics," even though the talk and action
often veered off into the specific areas of Civil Rights, or peace, or
the application of abstract concepts like freedom. But where there
was urgency, it was highly personal. Students talking about a
hundred-megaton bomb, about the awakening when "those ships
sailed toward each other off Cuba," or about the dogs attacking
the marchers in Birmingham, spoke not of news items but of
actual events being registered on their own consciences.

Yet many of the most seriously concerned students found little
satisfaction in the campus organizations. The Young Republicans
and Young Democrats seemed to be an every-four-years' explosion
to those not intimately involved in them, though their leaders were
often able and energetic students who actually did care about the
intervening three years. Specific efforts for demonstrations and
marches often ended in disillusioning the most thoughtful participants. "The wrong people rush in," one student said, "and the
whole thing gets garbled." He described a march the year before,
organized by the Student Peace Union. Some students carried

signs saying, "Stop All Bomb Testing." Others attacked the United States for its resumption of testing, while others advocated the Black Muslims. "Not exactly peaceful!" the student remarked, and went on to say, "You see why we have had it with marches and demonstrations." Yet their caring continued and had to be expressed in their talk, their reading, their studying, their local political work.

While the most politically-minded students were talking or struggling with their frustrations and their intellectual quests, others, equally alert to crucial issues in their world, were involving themselves in single-minded activity that presented fewer confusions, though not necessarily fewer problems, than a general interest in "politics." The tutoring of local children from culturally deprived areas, the ride to Jackson, Mississippi, and the voter registration, the drive for integrated housing or the preparation of the new international issue of the campus paper, these went on along with or independent of what students called "political concern." And surrounding all these efforts, these conversations and confusions, these stabs at "meaningful action," with these frustrations and ironies, were the rest of the students, understandably busy in programs stepped up beyond their expectations or right in line with them. They had little time left over for the other parts of that dwindling concept, "college life." Perhaps they felt more concern than their parents may have had as they read a special edition of the evening paper or heard an interrupting bulletin on television. They would be momentarily concerned, then fall back into their pressing busyness. The wonder is that there are even a handful (and I saw a good deal more than that) who can manage, intellectually and emotionally, to care, to wrestle, to try to win others' interest, and to try to come to terms with their own concerns and with some hard realities in the complex field of what is now "politics."

7

John and the
Precarious Program—
Ray and the Going Concern

Nobody is ever neutral about student government. If it is ineffectual it comes in for as tough an attack as it does when it is controversial or superbly right or wrong-headed. I heard the laments about student government drowning in its minutia of bicycle registration and lavatory maintenance. Yet there were also busy and intelligent students like the girl who explained why she took part in student government: "People ask why top caliber people waste their time on Mickey Mouse things like student government. Well, these are top caliber people around this table, excluding myself. I believe we wouldn't do all this if it were just Mickey Mouse." I heard the gripes about women's dormitory rules and the hopes for "awakening our students to some realities in the world." Some leaders talked of futility and others of their sense of exhilaration, of doing something that really mattered. The unelected derided and praised their elected student leaders.

Beyond all these contrasts remains my impression that student government can be a powerful force for bringing students closer to political and social realities beyond the college walls. There are ways to do this, ways that can explode in the administration's face and make headlines, ways that seem to work independently of deans, presidents, and trustees, and ways that act in harmony with the "they" in the administration building. There seems to be nothing automatic about whether the student leaders will concern themselves with parking meters or voter registration in Mississippi, or whether they will take one or the other of these interests and ride them constructively or explosively, or both, depending on who is calling the shots.

Student Government Is No Ivory Tower

The student leaders at Fields University were trying hard to take student government into a wider vision of the off-campus world and a fuller participation in it. As in all my visits to universities and colleges, I saw only the snapshot, the scene at the moment, with a good deal of background filled in by the people in the midst of the scene, and some flashes of plans and hopes for the future from those same people.

Although Fields University has a tradition for free exchange of ideas and opinions, it does not have a long tradition of student government concerns and relationships with the world beyond the campus. And, as my encounters with student leaders there suggests, leaders were not at all sure that their efforts and interests would be followed even the next year by the same emphasis in student government. Still, they were full of zeal to do the job, to drive for what John Kovak, the student president, called "getting a program going" as opposed to "messing with 'activities'."

John himself had been active in student government since he was a Freshman, and had been in and out of the state legislature projects involving tuitions, teachers' salaries, tuition grants and money for research, as these came up in state legislative committees. These experiences contributed significantly to his later work as student president, with its all-out drive to educate the campus in what he called "significant realities beyond the campus." He spoke of the attitude of the state legislators toward his early efforts:

A lot of the state legislature people were skeptical at first. Junior year was the year I gave most of my testimony in legislative committees. We spoke right after the chancellor, on loans and tuitions and

comparisons among universities. Some of the people were surprised at
us having all this information available. They realized this was not a
case of some kids shouting their mouths off. We tried to keep it
informational, person-to-person, and we still do this. It's not a matter
of marching and sitdown drives and spectacular things. It's a matter of
personal conversation.

The Mississippi Plan

John spoke about other efforts to reach out beyond campus
affairs. He spoke of an "educational campaign" and a fund-raising
job coming up. He mentioned three speakers from Mississippi:
Aaron Henry, governor candidate in the mock election of the
summer of 1963, who had received 80,000 votes; Art Thomas,
trainer for the students going down the Mississippi to help with
voter registration; and Fields U.'s preceding year's student-body
president now working for the NAACP. "We're after voluntary
contributions from students and from the houses," John explained. "We want to get the facts around. We want to see if we
can touch the social funds in the houses, give a big dance, sell light
bulbs for a day, paint house numbers with fluorescent paint on the
curbs at $1.00 a number. We'll find all sorts of ways to raise this
money."

The hope was to send Fields University students to Mississippi
with the money raised, to help with the education and registration
of voters during the coming summer. John was doubtful about the
students' attitude toward fund drives in general, but he was for an
all-out effort, with a hope from $1,000 from the faculty as well.

I asked if all this interest and activity were a tradition at the
University, if student government "meant" this kind of thing
there. "No," he said;

There's nothing automatic about it. Last year's student president was
a powerful fellow, and he saw the light—he's working for the NAACP
now, and his brother is a Sophomore and coming up in the leadership
here—at least I hope he is. And I can see the light on all this . . . and
some of us are knocking ourselves out to broaden the view of other
student government people around here. But all this is useless if we

can't get across to the campus as a whole. Our main effort is just that—a big educational job on the campus.

The Campus and the U.S. National Student Association

Fields University had been debating since 1950 as to whether to join the N.S.A., and it finally did in 1963. There had been a lot of talk about the cost. Some of the students wondered whether N.S.A. was leftist, or inefficient, or unrepresentative of student opinion, or "too remote from our concerns," or placed too much responsibility on the student delegates. But behind all these reservations were really two ideas: First, that N.S.A. might be some kind of alien, left-wing group; and second, that on-campus problems should come first, and not off-campus problems, whether local, national, or international. "Both of these ideas have been pretty shattered by now," John said, "but it isn't easy to shatter them."

"Who Cares?"

The most articulate dissenters to off-campus activities were four fraternity presidents. Their attitude was as defensive, even as defeatist, as the student government leaders' was forward-thrusting and confident. Their mocking "let's face it" tone suggested that the battle really had been lost, and all they could do was stick pins in the ironies and inconsistencies in the ideas and behavior of the present officers. They needled what they kept calling "intellectual idealism." Our conversation ranged from faculty attitude toward sports to drinking rules, from the remoteness of Civil Rights efforts to the futility of "getting carried away by principles." When the talk turned to some of the same themes I had heard from student government people, the contrast was striking. One of these men spoke of "the great loss in interest in student government around here. It's the direction it has gone—into off-campus things, international things, Civil Rights, all that." Another joined in, "They're trying to raise $5,000 to send people to the South to help register Negroes. I mean, who cares—registering voters thousands of miles away?" I sensed no hostility to Negroes or to the cause of Negro voting. The meaning seemed to be simply that the whole effort was about something so far away that it had no relevance to the fellow speaking or to the campus,

Another took up the theme: "There are more problems around campus that you see every day. We see parking meters moving their way in here farther and farther every day. This kind of thing gets five minutes worth of concern in the student government." Then the conversation shifted back to the Negro voter registration. "They"—evidently meaning the most vocal student leaders —tell us that if we don't help the Negroes, then nobody will. That's the angle they are trying to put over on us. Of course that's fallacious." The first one to speak came back into the conversation: "It's all too much. I was on the 'new' senate for a while, but it got too dull with all this off-campus emphasis." These four men were articulate on this subject, but were more so, and more interested, about campus problems involving student discipline, teaching procedures, and the current intellectual climate on campus. Ill will was quite absent from the actual tones and faces in this conversation. Rather, four seemed to be searching honestly and with some dismay, trying to fit what they saw happening on their own campus into their own scheme of things. They had none of the bitterness or suppressed fury I saw, for example, in the group of men at City University, who grimly agreed that "all we really want to do around here is make it hard for the liberals." These fraternity leaders at Fields may have been indirectly commenting on the loss of fraternity control of student government.

A Strong Student Government Group

If John saw his program at Fields as precarious, some of the other students I talked with elsewhere found theirs paralyzed. I heard some fairly savage talk about Mickey Mouse Club, and the defenses against these charges were not encouraging. One girl, after listening to a denunciation of the futility and triviality of what went on in student government on one campus, told me, "I am *on* student government, and I say all right, suppose what we do *is* Mickey Mouse. There's still some satisfaction in it. You learn how to run a meeting, how to get people together and coop-erate—that kind of thing. I find this valuable even if these others don't!" Other students on this and other campuses spoke repeat-edly of the danger of sticking their necks out, into or from inside student government. In fact I heard so much talk about "the futility of trying" that I wondered if in some cases the laments about apathy were not simply, as one student suggested ". . . an excuse. We talk about the apathy around here and the futility of student government. But maybe we just don't *want* student gov-ernment to do anything." Other students picked up the theme of trivia: "We get lost in codes and revisions of revisions of our requests for definitions of our authority."

Let us focus on some of the going concerns I saw, such as the exciting one at Fields and the thoroughly established, powerfully traditional one at Country State University. There the student president is paid $1,500 a year and usually carries a lighter-than-average course load, making up the credits in the summer or in a fifth year before graduating. This president, whom I shall call Ray Carradine, ran a major operation on the Country State campus. He was in charge of a $45,000 budget for student activities, and he was up to the ears in these activities, personally determined to bring them into a relationship with the major national and inter-national issues of the day. He had just been accepted for the Peace Corps when I arrived on campus, and was to leave for his training shortly after graduation, which was six months away. His succes-sor had the same kind of almost startling maturity and thoughtful-ness that Ray had, and he shared many of the same major goals for the University.

Ray characterized his own view of student government and his own experience in it:

We have a strong student government group here. It's pretty large and it isn't provincial. I get around to other campuses. I traveled something like 15,000 miles this year to see what they are doing and talking about and to get new ideas, and I have a pretty good chance to share these experiences when I get back here. It means a lot to get out and talk about some of the problems and realities around the country.

Most students have a very little concept of what goes on outside their own campus, and I think it's up to the student government to do something about this.

What I saw and heard from Ray and some of his associates was striking in that the student government was making a massive effort on campus to mix the large issues and the local ones, to "bring the word to the whole campus" about perspectives and concerns important to the student leaders.

Ray, Jane, and Gail on Student Government

Three student-leaders' efforts to avoid extremes and to do a respectable educational job on the campus plunged them into problems and complexities and ironies. Yet they seemed to handle these, at least on their good days, with some perspective and even humor.

Jane was the University's chairman of the National Student Association representatives, and Gail was active in the formation of a new campus political party. They began by wondering about their right to speak for the student body. Ray said, "We wonder if we should make recommendations about Civil Rights matters, for instance. So many of the students feel removed from anything off campus, and it's so easy to get provincial. But this is a large lobby, and the student government group is concerned about these wider problems, and we're trying to make the rest of the campus concerned—it *should* be concerned."

What followed was an interesting interweaving of the large and the trivial, the idealistic and the practical. The leaders speaking knew this was happening and were committed to the necessity of this interweaving. They started in on the campus political parties with Ray's comment:

The Greeks used to outnumber the Independents, 4 to 1, yet we have six Greeks and six Independents on the student governing board. The parties have all been done away with and are now reforming, plus a new one, and the Greeks and the Independents will have to reform if they are going to reform on residence lines. Up to now we needed two parties—there seemed to be no other group you could relate to besides the living group—fraternities or dormitories.

Jane was dissatisfied with having the campus organized around living groups:

We hope for more than *social* identification. There should be a stand or a viewpoint as the unifying factor that students could gather around, not simply the fact of how their living setup is arranged.

Ray was doubtful:

I don't think the student body is concerned about finding an issue to rally around. Their living units, if they are going to rally around anything, are the natural thing.

Jane got specific on "issues" and local, noninspirational intensities:

Well, there *are* issues: women's hours, the administration's control of students. Our new third party is progressive on student government and wants to deal with *every* area of student interest. We want to reach out for greater responsibilities for our own actions. Independent housing and co-ed housing are some of the things we're interested in. We're after a *community* of student interests.

Ray laughed and turned to me:

These two girls used to stand only on the great big issues—N.S.A., student rights, big questions, but they found that there was no interest in the students for these things. So it looks to me as if they had to lower their ideals to things students *can* care about. Women's hours, for heaven's sake! That's ridiculous. The A.W.S. can handle that sort of thing. Why bother student government with it, *unless* you are after strong student support. More student freedom? Sure, you can always get student support for that. You have picked the old student support issues."

Jane recovered with a more lofty vocabulary, at any rate, to offset the aura of "student support" issues:

I disagree with the present setup. Our view of a political party is that it can work as a pressure group. A political party *is* a pressure group. It's a link between student government and the masses of people on campus.

Ray pressed her:

You want student government to do big things. Students want to do 'me' things—not the National Student Committee for this or that. You're on shaky ground talking about the big things such as N.S.A., Civil Rights, and so on. These students don't give a damn.

But Jane continued the argument:

Women's hours *are important* in student responsibility. Living plans are important. During finals week a lot of us got together and figured we could afford to start a new party. I was the only Greek in this group. We're ready for something better than the solid Greeks versus the solid independents.

Ray had reservations about new groups:

People are not concerned with political philosophy. Those people that got together to start the party, they wanted to get elected. With the change now in their attitudes, they are divided into still another party. The fourth new party has no philosophy at all. They just want to be elected. There's a fifth one cooking and *it* wants to be elected.

At one point Ray spoke of Country State University as "a real little monastery." He explained, "The students are trapped here. The herd of 8,000 shuffling feet at one time can create a lot of dust. If the student government can't produce something intelligent and handle its role well, the administration is going to think about taking back all that responsibility it has passed on us." I asked how many students were actually involved in some kind of significant responsibility in the student government network at Country State. Ray's estimate was a surprising 650, and he added that four times that number apply to get on the various committees, of which there are fifty. "There are some faculty on student committees and some students on faculty committees and a collection of joint student-faculty committees," Ray said. "There's even a student on the Educational Policies Committee—the student vice-president sits on it." This sounded to me both promising and appalling, promising in the large number of students in government and working with faculty to get the something done, and appalling in the possibilities for red tape and minutia. Ray agreed with me:

Most student governments are bogged down in this red tape—what they *have* to do. We are hired as staff people on a regular salary. I am up here about five hours a day, writing letters, talking to people, going downtown to meet community agencies, traveling to other universities. As I sit here I feel those 150 eyes behind me. I know there's been good effort in student government around here and I want to keep it up." [The 150 eyes were in the photographs of previous student leaders that were on the wall behind him.]

However responsive or apathetic this or that mass of students on the campus might be, it seemed to these leaders that the student government itself, including those 650 students who were actively involved in some kind of significant effort, had responsibility that mattered. Jane spoke of how much the dean of students expected of the student government. "These expectations are high, and we try to perform along with these expectations." Ray spoke of the interest and *the ability to listen* of the University's president: "He listens with both ears—I mean he *listens*—he *waits* on student opinion." Gail added: "We have talked often to the president of the University. At one time he said 'If you want to get there fast, this is the way to move,' and then he planned an approach with us about what we were thinking about. I told this to people on other campuses and they were shocked that a university president and a student government could talk this way with each other." Jane emphasized that it wasn't just the University's president talking with a handful of leaders. She said it was crucial the way students, faculty, and administrators collaborated in so many different parts of college life. Ray commented: "Actually, maybe they *had* to give us responsibility. We were trapped here on this campus, miles from nowhere. They had to give it and hope for the best. But the point is that they *did*."

A problem comes up when administrators and students collaborate in making policies and carrying them out, and these leaders and other students I talked with were quick to speak of it. One recalled that the dean of students had been attacked once in twelve years "for controlling student government people. They said he was charming the student leaders in order to control them. The dean was deeply hurt about this. But the charge flashed around campus a day or so, and then faded away. In general you hear mighty little of this sort of thing." A committee member put this in: "There's a large administrative staff advising all these committees. I suppose that is a subtle influence filtering down from the administration on the attitude that the University wants to work with. But the point is that we don't feel maneuvered."

More of a problem than accusations of administrative control were the frustrations of the University administration's wheel turning. "This slowness drives us nuts," one boy said, "but maybe that's natural. And what saves the situation is that we feel they do listen to us." Ray was strong on this when he said to me, "If you want something bad enough, you can't say around here, 'We can't get it because we're students.' We take part, we're in more things, we see there's more to issues than simple blacks and whites. We get to see some of the real complexities and we can understand better a lot of things about the University than if we were standing on the outside banging for privileges and rights." One of his staff added: "We never get the finished decision. We get consulted, or if we do get a finished decision, it's justified and explained. We are educated in the committee system. We know we can get things better by this give and take, this listening and suggesting, than by banging on the wall of the administration building."

A Sign of Maturity

I heard some less wholehearted views on this campus than those of these three leaders, but I never heard the charge that the administration was brainwashing or controlling student government, except in the reference Ray made. And as I heard again and again from the deans and from the students about "the committee system," and the relationships it set up among students, faculty, and administrators, I realized how significant it was in bringing these three supposedly isolated worlds on a campus into communication. I don't know if the system insured the election of a leader of the quality of Ray or his successor, but something in the air made students like these three feel it was worth getting into student government and using their ability, drive, and vision.

Clearly they did not seem to be the type that needed the status of an elected office. And while Ray as student president followed the direction of his own concerns toward the Peace Corps and probably later toward a career in teaching, he was more resigned than enthusiastic about the idea of doing a patient and hopeful education job on his campus. It was not a matter of winning everyone to his own special concerns, but seemed to be more a realization that his responsibility as student president was to maintain a student government relationship with the whole campus as well as to coalesce off-campus realities and concerns with those of the campus.

Of the 8,000 students, Ray had said that 650 were actively involved in the activities committees, and four times this many were applying to get on them. Later he said that there were thirty students on campus involved in some kind of vital responsibilities and concerns that brought together this or that committee or activity, and he thought this was a good number. He made no apology for the things I might have heard or seen that could seem trivial, and he needed to make none, since his own view of these had been made clear:

I think it's a sign of maturity if the student government realizes there are things, piddling or not, that they must do in order to keep rapport with the student body, no matter how far out they may get on things that the student body thinks are remote from the campus. You can't stay just on the philosophical questions and concerns. If you do, the students get the idea that only God and the administration know what's going on in student government.

These students clearly refused to accept standard stereotypes for selecting those who fitted what kind of concern or project or approach to campus and beyond-campus interests. They were astute in seeing each other's style as well as in articulating their own vision of the campus and how it should relate to the world. They were, of course, exhuberant talkers and were enjoying themselves in their work—and it certainly was work—as leaders on this campus and in their talk about it. Students who had left college to serve full time on some front line of their special dedication might find these leaders' talk superficial because, compared to those who had given up college, the leaders weren't "doing anything."

If the measure of student sincerity or even of political and social maturity is that students leave college and join a barricade, then I suppose these and nearly all others of the most interested students I met on this study will be judged as superficially "concerned" talkers. Obviously, this measure is not fair to the students still in college. If they can reach out, as these leaders did, to make their education relate to more than courses and activities, if they can get some kind of perspective on the wider community that sustains them and allows them to take part in it, then surely their talk is more than a long and hollow bull session. These students think about long-range issues and movements and about their own participation in them. They have, rightly or wrongly, abandoned any hope or respect for student sign-carrying and agitating. Yet they are in touch in their own thinking with complexities and compromises as well as dramatic issues. They have learned something about individual idiosyncracy and group inconsistency, and they have had the experience, and value it, of conversing about these things, not only among themselves but also with educators on the campus. Their network of activities, responsibilities, and encounters nourish and encourage their own widening vision and the level of maturity on the campus.

8

A Student Personnel Staff Takes a Look

What happens when a personnel staff closes the doors, gathers around a table, and "meets"? What do they talk about? How do they approach their problems, not as they talk generally to a visitor, but as they hammer out the thorny issues and try to understand the trends on just one of the many college campuses in the nation? A chance for an inside view of a meeting of a student personnel staff was illuminating. Examples of just what some deans see and talk about to each other allow the reader "inside" in a way that too few commentators on the educational scene and too few deans ordinarily make possible.

The group I met with was clearly secure enough so that there seemed no reason for them to be especially guarded in their conversations before an outsider. They were experienced enough in their profession so that talking with each other made real communication and real understanding possible and abundant. These people were talking about their own campus, their own problems and challenges, in the midst of a packed day in a packed week. This was a campus on which there had *not* been any major explosion in politics or social action, yet where there was some tradition for political and social concern, and a relative freedom from administrative panic at the thought of what cause-minded students might do next.

The student leaders in power at this university were closely associated with the National Student Association, and a major interest on campus was a drive for money to send students to the South to help with Negro voter registration. There was no political activity (in the spring of 1964) beyond a general interest and enthusiasm for individual candidates and issues somewhere between the immediate left of Senator Goldwater and the immediate right of Senator Morse. As a kind of background briefing for the visitor, the dean of students and three of his staff began to talk about campus atmosphere for political and social action and attitudes. He had spoken of the influence of last year's student president, now working on voter registration in Mississippi, and of the resource the National Student Association had been to the young, idealistic leaders on this campus. I heard nothing of the idea that the N.S.A. had helped cause campus trouble by antiadministration and antidean activity. There was no way of keeping the irresponsibles from using N.S.A.'s educational program in some bizarre ways, but evidently the leadership at this university was serious and responsible.

The dean's view was: "It's more than N.S.A. providing issues and procedures. It's that students now seem to *want* to get involved with something important. Homecoming, big week ends, floats, proms—these things are out. Students are thinking of that sort of thing now as high school stuff." (I heard this again and again from students on this and other campuses, sometimes with the key term being "*junior* high school stuff.") The problems came in finding what was important, what was worth identifying one's self with. The dean said, "The Mexican Village project our students have, the voter registration in Mississippi, these things have come in vigorously in the past two years, and they are reaching quite a segment of the student body. Some pretty high-powered people have come onto the campus to talk to students, about Civil Rights mostly, and they've made a deep impression."

New Interests, New Forces

There began an exploration of the newness of this interest in major outside events and issues. The dean of men mentioned that the University was outdated in some respects, since there was still some hazing and discrimination in fraternities and so on, but that these problems were generally ignored because of the real crush for interest in the *outside* problems. Another administrator reminded his colleagues that, "It's always more tempting to get excited about the starving Armenians. There's no interest in the mundane, the seating at games, the week ends." Then he asked, "All this is within the past three years. Why?" The dean of men answered this one: "Well, I think Kennedy's election in 1960 was one factor. Then the visits of some of these powerful speakers. Then there's the new faculty that comes from the East and from Europe and the fact that we now have 500 foreign students enrolled. All these things have a big influence." The dean of students added, "It's in the explosion of the size of the university, too. There's a tremendous build-up in the staff of a lot of universities. There are more marginal new teachers, that is, marginal in their academic competence, and there are a lot of young Turks who are quite different from the old established faculty communities in a lot of places. We attract graduate students. There's a wonderful opportunity for reseach, especially in science. This gets people with little liberal arts background. It's harder to get good advisors out of these people. They realize that the mileage is in publishing and research. There's a model Republican convention coming. There's a political science professor giving a lot of time to this, but he says that he can't give too much or get too identified with this or his superiors will think he's not scholarly."

Student Control and Student "Rights"

A recent campus issue appeared to rankle this group of student personnel people. It was the passing of a new code of regulations in which students had new responsibility for enforcement and discipline. Student-faculty committees were set up, even a student-faculty court, and the dean of students and his staff were pretty much removed from this process. There was feeling that "the faculty or some of them have imposed this new student responsibility business on the students. Most of the students don't really

want it. Here's something new for them to be apathetic about."
Others saw the new code as tied up with the current interest in
"rights," anybody's rights, and specifically students' rights. The
deans would have less power over students, and students would
have more responsibility in a kind of elaborate "legal" structure of
their own, with some key faculty members willing to take part.

The problem seemed to be in students' hesitation to take part
and in desirable faculty's hesitation to take part, and in the removal of what some of the deans called "therapy" in a student's
case. This was explained in this way: "There's no *explanation*, or
discussion, or *therapy* of students in disciplinary matters now in
the new code. We think the therapy part is the more important
thing, not the punishment. There used to be counseling from the
dean, someone with experience and mature perspective on student
problems. This is in line with the educational objectives of the
institution. Now all this is removed from us. The students have
their own court, and the idea is to assign their own punishment.
The actual information is even kept from us, so we won't put it in
records."

Another added, "What we are saying is that the *process* of how
a student problem is handled is more important than the event.
They are saying the event, the facing up to the "crime," and the
treatment of it by the student court or the student-faculty court is
the main thing."

As I listened I could see that these people believed the idea of
"my rights" was something students had seized upon out of the
national struggle, a kind of identification with persecuted people, a
desire to join the fight for "rights" even when it was on home base
and the issue was something petty or just traditionally "disciplinary." (I had heard this on other campuses. One dean said that
the pseudo-legal elaborateness of one student's determined refusal
to give up his university identification card in a bar had caused the
university to issue a new identification card to all its students with
"Property of the University of ———" printed on the bottom.
Thus, when someone asked to see the card, the student could not
stand on his "property rights" and refuse to give or show the
card!) The issue was complicated here, however, by the fact that

few students were interested in this kind of local fight for students' rights. The deans felt this, and my conversation with students corroborated it. The main student leaders could not have cared less about wrangling over student disciplinary matters in old or new structures, but they did care about national and local matters involving what they called *"genuine* rights issues."

The New Court

But there remained students who *did* care about the campus wrangling and who saw these disciplinary issues as the major, most interesting, campus fight. "Those students were impressed when the new court suspended somebody," one dean said. "But, I'm not sure that suspension was the right decision. The court and some of the students may have felt it was an impressive move, but who is supposed to think about the student himself? I was worried about *him*, but I was not part of this whole business."

Other problems, involving the faculty role in the new efforts for student responsibility, came forward: "The faculty votes for the new disciplinary code, but when a problem comes up with an individual faculty member, he won't send the kid to the court because it's too complicated. He'll call up the dean of men and say, 'You handle it.' The same faculty member voted for the disciplinary code, which in effect was supposed to bypass the dean of men and put the things in the hand of the student-faculty court!" Someone mentioned a plagiarism case. "The kid admitted it in writing. Then the student leader of the court, the student chairman, spent 45 minutes berating the teacher and questioning whether he was qualified to recognize plagiarism when it happened!"

"Another example was a fraternity party. There was a pretty blood-curdling report by the party's chaperones, and it went to the student-faculty court for a hearing. There was an appalling grilling of the chaperones. Finally the lady chaperone was pinned down to all sorts of details that she had to spell out. A total of *eighty hours* was devoted to this!" The dean of women commented, "The sad thing was the disillusionment in student participation. One girl

dropped out of the court rather than go on. Then she dropped out
of school. One person who had helped write the code and was a
good student was urged to stay on the committee just for morale,
since everybody else seemed to be falling by the wayside."

The dean of students then made a surprising comment. At least
there seemed to be no preparation for it in what had been said. It
was this: "I think we could say that this all reflects an inadequate
preparation for a great step forward." Nobody had suggested that
the whole new concern about "students' rights" and the problems
with the student-faculty court was "a step forward." Yet this was
the dean's perspective, even as he recognized all the problems and
deplored the removal of the dean of students and his staff from
some crucial kinds of counseling and guidance that seemed particularly appropriate to them.

The group thought this over. Some could not accept it. Some
were willing to wrestle with it. The fact remained that even though
the student leadership was thinking about Birmingham, other
awakened students were thinking about "my rights" on campus,
and some students and faculty had seized on the drama and potential rallying power of this. Maybe this would some day lead to a
genuinely wider meaning of "student responsibility" in campus
affairs, and maybe it was the dead-end that some of the personnel
people saw it to be now. All could agree that the change had been
inadequately prepared for. But was it "a great step forward"? It
was, at any rate, one of many expressions of the new concern with
political and social issues, though for some students and some
deans, it was a rather irrelevant one.

Professors and Deans

There was some exploration of the split between personnel
people and teaching faculty in the University. These deans felt
that some of the new faculty, including teaching graduate students,
were unfamiliar with the social milieu of the community and the
state, and this made for some odd clashes with parents and community. "Other faculty," one dean said, "are jealous of the academic rank of personnel people. They don't think they should

have it." Others saw faculty members as considering the deans simply as baby sitters, standing in the way of the maturity of the students. "We're seeing a new type," one dean said, "who stands up at a faculty meeting and waves his research grant in the air and preaches about how bad it is to perpetuate the childish state of college students and how they must be *freed*." Such faculty were said to be highly critical of the personnel department's firing of twenty-seven students during the preceding year. "But," said one dean, "the faculty fired about 1,000 during the same year, simply by their cold-blooded approach to grades and numbers and names-without-faces."

All these new forces whirling around the campus made new problems for the dean and his associates, especially with parents and legislators who wanted to know, "What's going on down there?" The new rules and regulations, and the student-faculty court, were evoking more noise than the concern with Freedom Rides and voter registration, and the dean and his deans had to absorb this clamor as well as all the other kinds of clamor on campus. The dean of students commented, "Well, we believe in student participation and self-government. Years ago, we promoted the honor system, sometimes over the struggles of students who said they didn't want it. We've always been behind the students' *doing* more. Students have dragged their feet on these things for years, and now suddenly it's all swung the other way, and maybe too far. But what's happening is still within our philosophy. It's what we believe in, and we've got to do what we can to steer this responsibility, make it right, and genuine."

The final comments in the session reached into the special interest in national and international issues, which struck these people as new and significant. The conversation moved again away from the campus problems and into "the world": the eager interest in special service programs, for which special training (six weeks, two and one-half hours a week) was required for eligibility; the students involved in a school for the retarded; the explosion of interest in the national "Y" conferences and the apathy about the local ones; the tremendous interest in the Peace Corps ("We're writing about thirty references a day!"); the rising wave of student feeling that "there needs to be more to my life than just making a buck." Whatever the "meaning" of the threads in this conversation, however those threads would be woven together in the work of the personnel people and the whole campus community in this university, surely—at the very least—the talk across this particular table showed something of the complexity of the challenge to the dean and his colleagues. This complexity and challenge cannot be managed in headlines and television news spots. It may be a crucial development of the history of how our college students can lead a campus life that is, as one teacher said, "academically excellent and relevant to the world at the same time."

9

How to Be Nonparanoid though Dean

"Student personnel work" has a complex and powerful set of aims, headaches, challenges, hopes, and procedures on many college campuses. On some, the term carries a vaguely unacademic aura, as if it referred to some new kind of "extra," related to activities and discipline, which nobody on a really "mature" campus needed to bother about. I told one college professor of a comment City U.'s dean of students made to me: "When I came here in 1936 I was *the* dean of students. Last week, when I looked last, I had a staff of 180!" Even knowing that City U. had 26,000 students, my professor friend asked in amazement, "What on earth is there for them all to *do?*"

There is in fact *plenty* for them to do. Once a college faces the fact that a student as an individual human being needs more than classroom challenges, a printed behavior code and an academic transcript for his four years, there is a wide-open field of opportunities and problems into which the dean and his deans have to venture. The explosion of student interest and concern for political and social problems on some campuses, the gradual awakening to them on others, the relative sleepiness about them on still others, all comprise many crucial parts of the answer to the question, "What do they all do?"

My conversations with personnel deans of thirty-odd colleges and universities may give some perspective to the experiences in this study. To begin with, student personnel people obviously do not agree on "what to do about" political and social action and interest in their students. Each has a highly individual network of people and issues to deal with, and these do not yield easily to formulas and diagrams. One dean spoke of the "murkiness of a lot of this. You can get into things which the principle or the issue still doesn't clarify. They get submerged in so many variables, rumors, personalities—or you see yourself as students see you, some kind of conservative clod taking papa's place and saying, 'My God, you can't do *that!*'" Another spoke of the lack of tradition for political and social activity on his campus. "I have the feeling that the students wish the University would *arrive.* I wish something would happen and I think they do, too—something to break through this diffuseness. There's privatism everywhere. Even the fraternities have trouble getting any interest up, let alone any idea or concern or social issue!" One administrator said rather ruefully, "Things are pretty much set up in the minds of our students *against* concern and participation, and there is an administrative disposition to keep it this way. Last year there was some agitation among some students and faculty when the president gave an interview which included the idea that students should not be unduly concerned about doing things about politics and social action. He said that college was a time to think about things, to absorb, and that students should save the *doing* until later. This was the president's opinion, not his instruction, on how a college should be run. But still. . . ." Another said that *his* president was "so Gung Ho for social action that the personnel staff never gets in on any of it. The students hatch it all privately with the president."

The Dean: Conscience, Nerves, and Ulcers

Other deans have no worries about how to stimulate "concern." I even heard of a mimeographed paper circulating around several campuses which was headed, "Attack the Administration of Your Choice. Here's How to Do It." Some campuses see their irresponsibles taking a free ride on a valid issue, simply to make noise or trouble, or to escape their own academic responsibilities. Yet the same campus may have students who care deeply and are seeking the answer to their conscience's question, "What can I *do* about this?" What does the dean say to *them?* "Hire a bus and go to Birmingham," perhaps, or "Go back and get your thesis done"? The faces of the responsible and dedicated weigh as heavily on many a dean's conscience as those of the irresponsible or the apathetic. Each presents real challenges, not to speak of the huge cluster of other challenges raging around the dean's head, such as the alarm of the college president at the possible trouble students may run into in a trip to Mississippi.

The howl of the community about editorials in the campus newspaper, the assault on the dean's office to win some new concessions for women's hours or fraternity liquor regulations, the horror of the parents at a new set of regulations for dormitories which get across over strong protest from the deans, the trembling of the earth when fourteen students launch a spectacular crusade in a department store and say they "represent the student body of the University," the rallying power of the new chemistry instructor from Heidelberg who inspires the students to a concept of "freedom" which rules that the dean's administration is by definition a system of repressive and sinister forces blocking student maturity! These and a thousand other hot spots demand the dean's attention, dedication, judgment, idealism, and action. If he were completely passive, simply waiting for things to bounce onto his desk, he would be busy and harried enough. But personnel people simply refuse to be passive, "to struggle," as one man said, "with whatever the next damn thing is that jangles my telephone." They see themselves, most appropriately, as intimately involved with the education of the students. This idea is apparently unpopular among some college professors, college presidents, and college students.

How to take part in this educational process in a constructive way, suggesting without intruding, protecting the university and the individual student at the same time, separating the spurious issue from the genuine concern, helping students experiment and make mistakes which somehow will not be disastrous, working to develop a morale on the campus in which freedom and responsibility keep each other's company, all these challenges provide as tricky a network of tightropes as any diplomat has to negotiate, and surely more of a one than many a professor of Humanities 3 or Biology 4 has to walk.

A Real Issue or a Free Ride?

There is nothing new or exciting about the student assault on the hallowed tradition or rule, policy, or procedure. "The murkiness" that keeps some deans awake at night comes when some students see a genuine cause in an issue while others see in it a vehicle for a free emotional ride, to be paid for, one way or another, by the university. I heard a good deal about this from personnel people in and beyond the seven universities of this study. I have already quoted the dean of men at one university, who said that his campus' eruption over the Freedom Riders loan illuminated the campus, brought student government out of the doldrums of pettiness, and launched some meaningful conversation about important issues. This was his conclusion, even with the enormous amount of emotion, misinterpretation, confusion, and energy that the whole business had evoked. The *educational* worth of the experience far outweighed these effects. The dean saw himself as part of this educational process. He hoped to seize the situation and make it a useful experience, not just another campus problem to be hammered out. Other deans have spoken about the university's responsibility to *find* issues, whether or not students were finding them, which would bring "the world" onto the campus and challenge students to face and examine something important. One dean said the National Student Association had been of great value on his campus in doing just this.

The Four Too-Easy Propositions

It is easy to make quick assumptions about deans' prejudices and motives. A dean who thinks of political and social action simply as material for more campus nuisances is obviously going to have increasing nuisances to cope with. He will also drain off a good deal of the idealism and concern of his student antagonists in skirmishes on the campus barricades. And students who see "my rights" or "academic freedom" or Civil Rights work in the South simply as a club with which to "attack the university administration of your choice" are going to have their own satisfactions and frustrations, but these will not have much to do with the issue being contested. The truth is a good deal more complicated than any of the following four propositions, each of which is by now quite familiar, almost a cliché:

1. The deans want genuine concern for and participation in world realities and the students don't care.

2. The students have real concerns and the deans are too politically and socially conservative to respect or even recognize these.

3. Experienced and established deans find any student action that rocks the boat to be the work of campus irresponsibles.

4. Dedicated, awakened students with new determination to identify with "the world" in political and social issues find their efforts blocked and frustrated by the personnel department's red tape, hostility to change, and personal antagonism.

There is a good deal of satisfaction in any of these four propositions. I had no problem of finding students who would happily point to statement 2 or 4 as "our situation on this campus." But on the same campus I would find students who saw the issue as more complicated than a simple proposition, and who tried to face up to these complications. For the deans, there may be less temptation than for college students to see themselves in the misunderstood victim's role. Yet I saw campuses on which the most perceptive dean could easily describe his attitude by either statement 1 or 4—at least during some part of the year, or the day.

Who Speaks for the University?

An important issue on a number of campuses is whether a single student or a group of students has the right to say he or it speaks for a university's student government or for the whole student body. Actually, there is not much debate on whether such a student or group does have this right; an individual or a like-minded group is *not* "the student government," or "the student body," or "the university." But often the students, in the intensity of their zeal and in a sense of futility at what any individual can do, imply that their actions—their picket line, their petition, their rally, their invitation to a speaker, their march—"represents" or "is" the effort or feeling of the whole university. As one student said to me, "Why the hell does it *matter* whether or not we're an individual or a group or whether we're chartered or who we speak for and all that administrative nonsense? The issue is clear and I defy anybody on the administration to come out against the issue!" To such a student, the dean and his deans look pretty timid when they insist on establishing whether the student action is an individual matter or an expression of the university position.

One dean said, with some understandable concern,

Some of those students don't *want* to act as individuals. They're scared to death of an individual act. But they do want to be the individual who determines what "the mass" thinks and how "the mass" expresses itself. They want to write the university's record when it goes on record.

This dean put the problem sharply when he said,

If the university becomes involved in political things outside, it loses its freedom as an educational institution. Now many of us have said that it's important to stimulate concern about political and social problems and issues. Some think it's *so* important to do this that the University should allow students to do basically dishonest things. I call it basically dishonest, anyway, if a few students are allowed to say, "We speak for the student body in taking this position, in carrying out this action." Now some may think it's all right to let this go by if it stimulates the right kinds of concern. I say the end does not justify the means.

Others have argued that the educational values of having students involved and concerned are so great that university administrators should not block the expression of these concerns regardless of how haywire the extremists may be. This same dean said to this:

> The element of concern is so often an emotional state in which people take leave of their ordinary values. The end is thought so valuable that people resort to any odd means. It all comes close to a real kind of hysteria. The manipulators, the students who go in for political intrigue, take advantage of this and ride it. My question is, "Does the positive educational value coming from all this justify the wear and tear, the hysteria, and the basic dishonesty when they happen?"

Complexities Within Complexities

Readers of magazine articles on the splendid new political and social awakening of college students, or on the alarming new wave of hot-headed rebellion among campus organizers, are missing some of the complexities that some of these deans and students are actually facing. Often it requires delicate probing before the deans can discern which are the "political manipulators" and which are the sincerely concerned students. It is not always clear which kinds of student political manipulation among students are necessarily good or bad, sincere or insincere, for what university at what time. Concerned students are torn by personal loyalties and friendships, by a feeling that "the issue is all," while at the same time understanding the relative conservatism of any *institution* about speaking out and acting on political and social issues.

I had conversations with students in which they grilled me with care about this study and its auspices before beginning to tell me about their own interests or actions in politics or Civil Rights. Yet these same students had either been asked personally by one of the deans if they would be willing to talk with me or, in some cases, gone to a dean with a special request to take part in one of the conversations. It is possible, evidently, for students to think of an administrative "they" as "hatchet men," "fogies," "enemies of students rights and freedoms," and repressive stooges while they maintain good personal relations with and respect for key men and women within the "they."

A dean and his deans are frequently stuck with too little or too much of the new political and social concern among students. But the ones I have talked with are clearly committed to having a constructive part in this new reality. "My God, what next?" is clearly not adequate. Neither is preoccupation with large-looming problems of campus sex and alcohol. Similarly, neither is the intricate network of activities, though it is clear from my campus visits that a very real strength for many important educational values in and out of political and social concerns lies in the relationships and working together of students and personnel people in activities programs that mean something to the life of a campus and which assume significant decision making and accountability from students. "We used to fight the kids," one dean said to me. "It was a constant battle about who could get permission to come and speak on campus, or some such issue. If you're going to fight them, resist everything that they suggest in the political and social action business, all you're going to do is spin wheels. Now we try to help, and students come and ask for help."

This is a hopeful start. It is the two-way communication between students and personnel people that impresses me so much in what I have seen, even when a campus was exploding or when it was asleep to political and social concerns. If there is this communication, or the beginning of it, plus the conviction on all sides that the personnel people stand as educators and not road blockers, something important and useful can come out of this new campus ferment, for our colleges, our students, and our society.

10

The Greeks Speak Up

The days when the fraternity people got the elected jobs and then the appointed jobs are gone. The house can't keep a hold on a lot of campus activities. I couldn't even perpetuate my fraternity brothers in the Carnival this year. Fraternities are separated more and more from the campus community. . . .

This one theme sounded above all others among fraternity and sorority people. Dwindling power and influence of "the Greeks" is a reality that belongs in any discussion of political and social action on campuses. If many fraternity-sorority people feel that their relationship with campus life is less active and influential than their older brothers and sisters remember, it may be because they stand somewhat aloof from campus stirrings in political and social concerns, and this removes them more and more from influence on the changing campus.

One of the most illuminating conversations I had with fraternity men showed a series of steps and problems that is crucial to this study. The two young men, in this conversation were evidently interested and influential in the fraternity picture. They were also effective and agreeable people. One came from the West, one from the Southeast. They began with what had become a familiar theme: that much political and social action on campus was radical rabble-rousing, giving a false image of the college life. And with this came another key theme: the disappearance of the "real" college values, what one called the "healthy" aspects of college life. They worked from these themes into other more complex ones as they defended less and explored more their own dilemmas within the fraternity. The Western student was talking about the political activists on campus:

You get a lot of rabble-rousing extremes around here in political action. This is no good for the University. This is the unhealthy kind of thing, it seems to me. The Young Socialists want to make trouble. I don't know why in a state university these people so easily get into the picture. You know it's distressing to be quizzed on "all that Communist business" when you go off campus. Reporters come onto the campus and take pictures of these extremists. It seems to me that the University's office of public relations doesn't direct the press to the *healthy* part of the university life to counterbalance these fringe things. They could cover the election of the student body officers or student activities like the Carnival, but no, they come and give a lot of publicity to the Freedom Rider loan in which we were trying to convince ourselves we should lend money to these people who had gone on the Freedom Ride that summer. Then you hear the public reacting about "those radical kids" again.

The other student got a word in on the proposed loan for the students who had gone on the Freedom Ride and had heavy legal expenses: "There's a minority in favor of the Freedom Riders. Yet *Time* said that the University *advocated* the Freedom Rides. It's very irritating to be stuck with the opinions of these few people as if the whole University agreed with them."

His friend spoke up for "the good things":

The University is not doing its fair share to point to the good things, even to *exploit* the good things. You hear this business of the "little red school house" from alumni all the time. You hear about the riots against the House Un-American Activities Committee. You hear these things and you get the impression that there's nothing but a bunch of wild-eyed Communists around. But there are things that people could pay attention to—good constructive things, the Carnival, the Spring Sing, Homecoming. Yet the press comes in eager to take pictures of some Black Muslims selling their papers out on the campus. The press could cover healthy things like fraternity water fights and college activities down in the village. These are just as much a part of growth and life and maturity on a college campus as picketers.

There was no grimness, no militancy for political conservatism in the comments about liberal causes and attitudes. There was genuine dismay at what seemed to be unfair emphasis on undesirable behavior, and unfair ignoring of "healthy" behavior.

I had met students here and elsewhere who would have been aghast at the idea of "healthy things like fraternity water fights" as suitable events for press coverage. The fact that these two fraternity men could talk this way with no self-consciousness about how some of this sounded in relation to the currents running across college campuses these days may show something of their fraternity's (as well as their own) insulation from some powerful campus realities. The Westerner went on:

Here's the business of the unhealthy things versus the good sound solid things about campus life again. Carnival represents the culmination of a big project which has to do with the ability to work with people and which has a philanthropic "in," too. The program is designed to give the University a really good, healthy activity and to keep some of the good traditions alive. And, too, it's to do something good for the community and have the community know about this, since we raised $30,000 to support the University philanthropy, which is a camp. It's the University's religious conference that runs this camp for underprivileged children. It's nonsectarian, but it's religiously based. There's been a fuss about this, too, as to whether the University can support something that is tied up to a religiously based organization. So, actually, it isn't the University Carnival—they get around it by words. But this experience gives us a material reward. It gets students together and gives them an activity and does some good in the community.

The Outside Ones

The commuters and outsiders seemed to be sources of trouble. There was, again, no hostility when one of the men said, "The residence halls are the source of the picketers and agitators. They feel alienated. The commuters feel alienated and the residence hall people feel alienated and that's where the activity comes from." The other spoke about this alienation. Suddenly shifting its meanings to include how any of the students could feel, not only the non-Greeks, he said: "There seems to me to be an awful lot of away-from-each-otherness around this campus, instead of togetherness. A lot of us have the image of a leaf-covered campus in the Middle West with five hundred students on it, and most of them sitting around in small groups or in professors' houses talking about things."

This "alienation" led to campus friction: any and every non-Greek group against the Greeks. The fraternity men mentioned the required pledge to end discrimination by a fixed date, and spoke of the fraternities and sororities that were holding out and those that weren't. I heard little on the subject of discrimination at any of the campuses from fraternity-sorority people. The edict to end discrimination was simply listed as one of several problems the Greeks were struggling with: "There's defeatism in the fraternities. The demand about discrimination, the ban on hazing, more control from the administration, the growing strength of the university residence halls and dorms—maybe it'll be someday like the fraternities at Barton U.—you know—the fraternity is just on a dorm floor."

A Shift to Something More Personal and More Complex

Even as these students spoke of this defeatism, something more personal, sounded in their words:

Our fraternity is lackadaisical. But I think there's a deeper problem. There's a conformity settling into mediocrity and a dislike of those people who go beyond this mediocrity. Often the people you want most in the fraternity don't even come to rushing. This is very hard— to see the good people more and more *not* coming to the fraternity. Then somebody works hard and is struggling to get good grades or really learn something and the rest say, "Oh come on, don't work so hard. Ease up. Take it easy." They're hard on the fellow that won't accept group norms.

The speaker paused a minute, then went further:

The trouble is there's so many sides to this. Being in a fraternity helps develop your personality. This is good, but it can kill the spark of a person. Maybe as a result of being in a fraternity you live better in the world, but still this spark is dead.

He was really trying to get at something. He seemed to be divided in himself about the values in learning to live with people in the fraternity style, conforming to them, and learning how not to stand out in the wrong way. It may "develop the personality" and "make you live better in the world," and yet he recognized the danger of "killing the spark."

His friend listened, then seized the new theme himself: "In our fraternity bull sessions, we talk a lot about complacency. Actually it takes a real *ability* to put up with mediocrity. We develop this ability. We're satisfied with the status quo. The incoming students are less mature." Note the contrast with the general feeling of upper classmen who spoke so admiringly of, or were so awed by, the new crop of freshmen. Where were these at rushing time in the fraternity? "The freshmen need longer adjustment time to the social and intellectual life. The people that come to us in rushing are less dynamic and less self-sufficient than they used to be. I was this way when I came to college. I couldn't exist on my own. I *had* to have the fraternity." This comment underlined the apathy problem: "I don't think that we *subdue* the extrovert in our fraternity. It's just that there's no interest in things especially." The other agreed. "Our fraternity is just not enthusiastic about *any* participation in student activities. We used to be active in everything, but we've just sort of drifted away."

At this moment I had the feeling that neither one of these men wanted to go any further in that direction. I don't think it was the presence of a stranger—even a stranger with a pencil in his hand—since their talk had been open, frank, and lively. I felt rather that they themselves hadn't pursued the matter in their own thinking and did not want to now. They recognized some personal problems of living in the fraternity, and that was enough for now. They moved back into the more comfortable topic of the decline of customs and traditions, a less personal subject, and the conversation ended after this note on traditions, hazing, morale and administrative pressure:

The fraternity paddle seems to me an instrument to forge unity. Yet we're told we can't have hazing any more, and I think something really goes out of the life of a fraternity when you take the fraternity paddle out of the hands of upper classmen. The military academies manage this very well, I think, because they get a real morale and a real unity. Our pledges used to get a real unity in that they as a group could, after their pledge semester, shift to being the one to wield the paddle on the incoming pledges. A lot of my fraternity brothers don't agree with this, but I think this has a lot to do with unity and morale in a fraternity. Yet all hazing is out now. If you tell somebody to drink a glass of water and he thinks the water is too cold, he reports it, and this is hazing. . . .

Other Themes

These men did not speak for all the fraternity-sorority people by any means. But they spoke for a good many of them. Others were frankly and consistently defensive about their house's image: "There's a lot of propaganda in the high schools about fraternities and sororities—as if we were all drunks and spent our time fooling around with secret rituals . . . ." I heard little about discrimination. Maybe this was too sore a subject in some houses, or was something that was moving toward a solution in others. I heard very little anti-Negro sentiment from fraternity and sorority people. In one conversation, one man in the fraternity lounge came out with a rather heavy-footed comment about Negroes, and the other men met it with an embarrassed silence. Then someone picked up the conversation and carried it in a different direction. One head of an intersorority group spoke rather grimly of the attacks on the sorority by CORE, followed by requests for help to get CORE established on campus: "CORE attacks us, so we're not about to support *them*. It's hard to talk back about discrimination to CORE when they attack us on these things, although they're wrong. It's just that you have to have a unanimous vote to take in a new member—I mean, one person can block things . . .," and she shifted to some of the extensive service activities of the campus' sororities.

I found little interest in discussing political and social concerns among fraternity-sorority people. I was careful to leave the topics for discussion open when I visited a house. The one time I did not set up my own introduction, my host said to the fraternity group, all of whom had been most cordial at dinner: "Our visitor will stay around in the lounge to talk about political interests such as Civil Rights, Communist speakers, Project C in the legislature, some things like that." At this nearly all the men fled. The fraternity president stayed out of duty and a sense of embarrassment at the exodus, and I immediately moved off any of these topics onto the particular fraternity and its characteristics and interests. This lightened the atmosphere, and a few of the men, seeing and hearing bits of the conversation, came back into the room and talked for a half-hour or so. They were fiercely proud of their fraternity and delighted to talk about it, and about "the identity you find here." I heard that phrase again and again, even more among sorority women than among fraternity men. They described the elaborate annual party for which they were doing decorations. These were a handful of impressive and enthusiastic men talking, relieved at the change of topic, eager to get in a good word for their house. One stressed an interesting idea that was new to my conversations. Instead of discussing what I began calling to myself the "Decline of the Greeks," they spoke of the differences among the fraternities and sororities on campus and the "emphasis on diversity" in their own house. They thought of other houses as emphasizing some special characteristics or qualities or interest. "But ours is interesting because we disagree a lot—some want one kind of new Freshmen, others want another kind. This makes things lively and varied here. You can really find your identity here." No one mentioned any of those topics the fraternity president had included in his introduction of the visitor.

Thousands of Miles Away

Occasionally I heard about the "oddness" of the non-Greeks. Interestingly enough, I heard about this from some nonfraternity people, too. One said: "There's more rah-rah in the fraternities, more seriousness in the upper class dormitories and in the off-campus students. The off-campus people can afford to be odd. The largest Peace Corps group is off-campus." This "oddness" evidently was related to involvement in political and social concerns.

Such concerns were remote from many of the Greek houses, but not from all, and not from every individual in any one of them. There was the fraternity president, one of four with whom I talked in an extended group conversation (see Chapter 7), who said, "The student government people are trying to raise $5,000 to send people to the South to help register the Negroes. I mean, who cares—registering voters thousands of miles away?" Some anti-fraternity stereotypes would suggest that the people in the houses would *condemn the effort* to raise money for this purpose. The reality in this case was somewhat different: "who cares" and "thousands of miles away." The same group of men saw a need for focus on immediate campus and community problems, the very same problems that the student government on that campus (and on others) found so insignificant: "There are more problems around campus that you see every day, *not* thousands of miles away. We see parking meters moving their way in here farther and farther every day. This kind of thing gets 5 minutes worth of concern in student government." Echoes of the student president who furiously denounced the preoccupation with bicycle registration and lavatory maintenance reverberated in this same group in the critical talk about "the kind of idealism prevalent around the campus," and the comment, "They say if we don't help the Negroes, no one will—that's one angle that they try to put over on us. Of course that's fallacious."

A Different Attitude

A few Greek members spoke of their house as a center of intense excitement and interest in many world currents. On a small campus, a man spoke of some of the things his fraternity had arranged for evening sessions. "The house sponsored a panel of professors to talk about Cuba. It sponsored a showing of Operation Abolition with an American Civil Liberties Union man and a John Birch man to discuss it afterward. The place was packed for this—they were hanging from the rafters. We had a session on the penal system with a prison chaplain, a psychology professor, a philosophy professor, and a man from the police department.

There was a discussion of the future of the "Radical Right" with a California congressman, with various Rightists, with a reformed Communist who became an F.B.I. agent and who then became a Bircher, an A.C.L.U. man, and a local Democratic politician—the moderator was an economics professor who blew up at the congressman's interpretation of Keynes! About twenty-five came for the prison one, but about two hundred came out for the rest, and the biggest one was the session on Operation Abolition." He stopped to give some setting for all this. "This kind of fraternity initiative and interest is pretty much the exception among the four fraternities on campus. Out of the four, two would *never* do such a thing, and one, even though it has a lot of live wires in it, just doesn't."

On the larger campuses there was less readiness for controversy and excitement about political and social concerns within Greek houses, though a number invited professors to meet with students socially and then talk about some special topic afterward. This was described by some as evidence of the new intellectuality on college campuses. One man said, "In our fraternity we have a guest speaker on Monday nights, someone from the faculty. We had Professor O'Connor come and talk on fraternities and that kept us going two months! You know, four years ago, you'd suggest a faculty speaker for the house and the men'd throw food!"

Across the campuses I heard this same kind of opening-up. One said rather plaintively, after describing an exciting evening fraternity session with a business law professor on existentialism, "Then we asked a political science man and he refused. He said he hated fraternities and that it was too late to do anything about them!"

Individual members of Greek societies saw themselves as holding views quite different from those of their friends in the house, in relation to current political and social problems. On campuses where many fraternities and sororities still had interior cohesion and high morale, if not campus influence comparable to "the old days," these individuals would obviously be working tactfully in their houses to encourage thought and discussion about some key political and social problems. A good example was the probing student in the fraternity discussion of the attacks on the university in Chapter 3. I listened to conversations, with people like him dropping a prodding question or comment now and then, in which there was serious exploration of political and social concerns, sometimes as a matter of course, sometimes apparently for the first time. In general, the first obligation seemed to be for the men (more than the women) to disassociate themselves from "campus oddballs with beards and picket signs." They seemed to accept the fact that world political and social currents did belong in their thinking and their talk. But "world" currents meant international explosions: "Back when those ships were steaming toward each other off Cuba, everyone was all excited. We listened to the radio day and night." National or local currents often seemed either trivial or perhaps important but vaguely puzzling: "Just politics." And, in general, these topics were not much in the conversation at dinner "after all day being intellectual in the classrooms."

A fraternity or sorority student probing and questioning from within may have made an impact on these groups. But I wonder if there could have been, and if there should or should not have been, any effort to bring fraternity men into the central campus events of recent years, as in those community attacks on the University. And, if so, who was to do it? The administration? Concerned faculty members? Student government leaders? How much should the fraternities on a campus be consciously informed, "educated," by other campus influences? Would this be interference, intrusion? Would the effort be used by the attackers as further evidence of "brainwashing the students?"

One thing is clear: Many fraternity and sorority people are ready to share some serious concerns. They recognize the decline of the Greek influence on campus and are ready to stop fighting it. They look respectfully on the changes toward more seriousness and more scholarship on campus. Yet they seem in an isolated pocket on campus, rather out of touch. They seem conscious of this "alienation," as some had called it, wondering if this was right or inevitable or if they would have to be "like those odd characters" if they *did* come out of this isolation behind the Greek ivy.

A final echo is a good one with which to end comments on the Greeks' influence on campus and still leave the subject reverberating. It haunts me as much as any of the student comments I heard. This is the voice of a young assistant in the student personnel department of one of the universities:

Some of the really creative, contributing students—juniors and seniors—are leaving the fraternity and getting apartments of their own. They say they've *outgrown* the fraternity. Yet the new students don't get the enrichment and maturity from these older students, the mature ones who have already had it with the fraternity and have gone on. And we just stand by. We know there are things to do, but we get so easily swamped in activities and headaches. But we can't kid ourselves—there are a thousand unused opportunities for education in the dorms and fraternities and we haven't even *started* to take hold of any.

11

What About the Faculty?

I heard very little about the role of the faculty in students' discussion of their interests in political and social concerns. I suspect that college students are glad *not* to think of who is "influencing" them. Most of them rather naturally see themselves as choosing among the forces, experiences, and people around them and developing a self of their own making. It is possible that the faculty or individual faculty members have more of an influence on students in *developing or inhibiting* various kinds of political and social concerns and actions than the students I talked with gave credit for. Certainly, some deans and administrators on the campuses saw and spoke up for both kinds of faculty influence on students.

Discussing the influence of "the faculty" was a very different thing from discussing student's interest in individual faculty members. I had the impression that even the slightest sign of "off-the-podium" humanness in a professor was seized on by students with greatest appreciation. Even without this slightest sign, students found that observing their professors' ways of thinking and acting on important questions was a fascinating study. The Havilland College material described some of this. Students' fascination with some professors' beliefs and attitudes there did not seem gossipy or carping. Students simply cared a good deal *what* and even more *how* some of the professors thought about *anything,* not only religion or the relation of religion to their academic subject. The "Ferment" groups at Havilland College (see Chapter 2) were an exciting example of what can happen on a campus once even a few professors are drawn into some kind of real, nonclassroom dialogue with students about anything from Communist speakers to legalized abortion. Some of the best discussions there, I gathered, had to do with key books, like B. F. Skinner's *Walden Two*, and often it was a book or article, rather than a general subject, like Civil Rights or the gulf between the generations, that launched the liveliest groups. But even here the problem was to get the faculty mainstays into the conversation, or even into the room. The young man who spoke wistfully of ever getting his department chairman to talk about anything seemed to take casually the presence of what he called "the campus gadflies" among the young faculty who showed up at the discussion groups. The nongadflies seemed to hold more real interest. I saw special excitement about professors who had never been to the discussions and who were just beginning to take part this year.

The Ivory Faculty Club

On the big campuses I heard the same kind of talk about individual professors; eager appreciation for the professor who was, as one girl said, "One of the few professors who will get off their fence now and then...," and a feeling of disappointment on up to fury about the professors who, as one boy said, "won't take a stand on anything." He explained, "This is so different from what I expected when I came to college. You never see a letter to the editor from a professor. They've taken no stand on any issue on this campus that has amounted to anything." Yet even a student speaking that way would immediately jump to the Exception with special appreciation. The Exception was usually beleagered in some way: he was a poetry professor who had volunteered to be sponsor for the Young Socialist Alliance, or a powerful personality who cared about students and was trapped in the publish-or-perish struggle and whose appointment was threatened.

I saw a major difference from campus to campus on what students thought the faculty's interest was in political and social issues. The boy quoted above had a good many other students whom I met at the same university to corroborate his view of a faculty which let students down by taking no stands on anything and evading all issues. I met personnel people and some powerful professors who agreed that this was the general situation on the campus. Yet the students I was talking with were the small group of concerned, caring ones who felt that something was very much missing. And the dean of students there made clear that this group was very small, indeed, and that he himself was concerned that the rest of the student body was so indifferent. This dean put a lot of stress on what the faculty was *not* doing: "The faculty is really schizo here. The emphasis is on research. There's great enthusiasm for federal grants, particularly those to scientific research. Yet there's the responsibility for *teaching* in the picture somewhere."

I heard of faculty meetings where the question of the proper mix between teaching and research would get a few minutes' airing. But the conversation seemed to stop with the professor's assumption that "my discipline comes first." It's not too far from that, if a man wants to travel that way, to "I don't want to waste time on kids and their activities and their discussions." A teacher, once he's on this all-out commitment to his *field*, gets his recognition from people in his field, across the country. He's not especially related to his colleagues on his own campus. His commitment separates him not only from students but also from his campus institution. One administrator spoke of teaching applications from young men, asking in effect, "How little teaching can I get away with doing?" The ideal seemed to be a professorship with no students. This administrator noted his worry that the faculty never asks *what* the University is trying to *do* with the students, in its curriculum and in its whole life."

Another university's story showed that the faculty was way ahead of the students in political and social awareness. There were some problems in this, and some disagreement on how desirable the faculty efforts were. Some students spoke appreciatively of the faculty's drive to get the students involved. But perspectives on styles and personalities differed. I heard several times of the kind of professor, usually young, who made a good deal of taking his meals in the Student Union and not in the Faculty Club. It was some professors on one campus who gave the students the impetus for a new discipline code, rather than the deans. Some professors had pushed harder for it than some students did, and the deans questioned the wisdom of the code from the start. The deans had had their say on this to me (see Chapter 8), only to add to the complexity of the questions: "How can faculty most constructively come out of their classroom, if they *are* going to come out of it, and affect student life and attitudes?" And, "What kind of impact is possible for them to make *in* their classrooms?" These questions are not often heard on some campuses, since it is generally agreed that professors will not "come out of their classroom" because of wariness or indifference or of commitments to other things, and life inside their classrooms may or may not have anything to do with the life that students care about with any convictions.

Throughout the study, I found far more impatience, not to say despair, with the professor who wouldn't commit himself than with the professor who was trying to indoctrinate. I heard practically nothing about the latter, supposedly such a threatening figure to some parents and community viewers-with-alarm. So often a special figure took over the conversation. University administrations often find these student-supported faculty stars a problem. Even as I write these words, I note in today's newspaper still another news story about students picketing for a popular professor whom they value as a teacher and whose promotion is being withheld because he has not come through with the proper amount of research. At least this is the way the story has reached the papers. College administrators bemoan the fact that sometimes these great issues, seized upon by the press, whirl around the head of a genuinely incompetent man, surely the wrong person to carry the banner of *the importance of teaching students* in a college.

But more often the issue is over a man or woman whose support comes from capable students and colleagues, from people with more than a sentimental spirit of rebellion to carry them through the demonstrations, rallies, petitions, and midnight conversations. It seemed clear to me that the students I met were so grateful to see the professor as a thinking human being that even if he did not recognize them, the students, as individuals in their own rights, the professor was still interesting, important, and useful. But if the professor went beyond his own willingness to commit himself on major issues, in and out of class, and committed himself to some kind of actual *encounter* with students, the response from students was extraordinarily appreciative.

If students did not discuss the "influence" of the faculty on student attitudes and actions in political and social matters, they did discuss processes of teaching, which seemed to me related, sometimes directly, to students' style of thinking and acting on their own. There was a great deal of talk about *freedom* in the classroom on many of the campuses. The meanings for freedom in these conversations appeared somewhat different from the meanings for the word when students were waving it in the face of a dean or college president about dorm rules or busses to Mississippi. The freedom that seemed threatened at Mountain University was repeatedly described as "freedom to ask questions, to talk up, in class and out." One student there spoke of "how wildly lucky we've been in our faculty—in the excitement of what goes on in certain classes." And there was the Mountain U. man in the fraternity discussion who spoke of the "freedom to stand up and scream if you want to." Many of these students were seeing this kind of freedom with sudden nostalgia, perhaps a sudden clarity. The absence of this freedom was bitterly mocked by students on the various campuses. "We have a special program for bright students here—very experimental. But the people who are running it don't listen to students' suggestions or concerns."

On one campus this problem was vigorously discussed in a social science class with the teacher present. The teacher was obviously sympathetic to the student's exasperation, and listened with care as students spoke of "the way some professors tempt students by setting up the beginning of a real discussion—you know—round table, ten students, the seminar bit—in order to discuss some policy or question, and the profs listen or pretend to listen and then reject it all or ignore it all." Later on, I heard more on this subject of a special program for bright students, including this comment: "We're beginning to get resigned to the possibility that this special program may be a publicity pitch—*another* one. The idea was to attract a special group of bright students and give them the best professors. Well, they didn't get the best professors —they got mostly the good students. Some of us have tried to organize this special group of students into some kind of active group on campus, active about *anything*. But none of them wants to do anything. They're scared of losing their scholarship, for one thing. They think it's better to just cooperate and play it safe."

On the other hand, when I talked over this new program with some teachers and administrators, I heard from them how disappointing it was to run an experimental program with students who were so careful, so timid, so ready for backbiting among each other in discussion and study. One most impressive professor was really exasperated at this missed opportunity. He saw the students as so awed by their inclusion in the special program, so anxious to sound bright and academically sophisticated, that any really significant encounter with the subject, with each other, or with the teacher was impossible. Clearly, the professors and the students were not in communication about the program, since each camp had such positive ideas about what was wrong with it, and these ideas would have been utterly strange to the other camp if it were to hear them.

The failure in communication so easily leads to careless blaming on both sides. Students will often seem to be ready and eager for some significant learning, which they say is blocked by the professors. And the professors, with equal sincerity and intensity, will speak of their frustration in trying to launch some significant learning in their program when students are to wary, too arrogant, too afraid of being wrong or naïve, or too unwilling to commit themselves, too obsessed with their own "objectivity," a screen for intellectual and emotional timidity. In the very few conversations I had in which students and faculty were both present, these assumptions could have been instantly challenged by both sides. Yet even this rarely happened, and probably *cannot* happen unless both sides make an effort to tell each other what it is like to be in each one's spot: what it is like to be teaching this course with these objectives and resources and problems, and what it is like to be a student in this course, in this college, at this time.

Too often students and professors, when they do meet together, do not seem to communicate their own experiences at all! They struggle to assume each other's frame of mind. The professor will strain to show that he "understands" and identifies with students, sometimes before he has even heard what the students are thinking and feeling. Or the students will strain to talk what they think is the professor's language, complete with elaborate "objectivity," the lingo of the specialty, and a smiling condescension for emotion and value judgments. On campuses where I encountered faculty and students with such different views of what was the matter with the adventure of learning in this or that course, I wished again and again that some professors and students would simply get into a room together and take turns listening to frank and honest talk about what it felt like to be a teacher or student on that campus, and what might be done to make the experience of "education" better. But even though it may be easy to say that the professor should cut through these personality defenses and seize the initiative, he would get nowhere if the students would not meet him with their own vision and concerns and language. Nor would students' "seizing the communications initiative" get anywhere if they approached a professor who found himself threatened by an encounter that might put him off his podium or out of his outline.

Real Learning and the Numbers Game

The large size of universities or of classes is obviously not the only problem removing students from faculty influences. Nevertheless, size is a major problem, and it came in for some comment: "How can you have anything really personally stimulating happen to you in a class of three hundred? Do you know, you could go through here for four years and be Phi Beta Kappa and never *once* meet and talk with a teacher!" On another campus I heard the same complaint, even though there were about 25,000 fewer students on it than there were on the other: "The numbers inhibit any real discussion, any real learning." There were seventy-five students in this speaker's class, mostly political science majors. The professor had told them he could not discuss with such a big group anything that was not in the text, and according to those students, he didn't. Yet, as one student rather plaintively said, "You need discussion of some of this stuff—not just heaving in answers." Another described the kind of discussion wanted: "You need to react to an idea and to watch yourself reacting, and then see how what you say strikes the others—see what happens to the idea as it gets passed back and forth." This may be asking for a lot in any classroom, especially one with seventy-five students in it, let alone one with three hundred. But the student who said this was making a crucial point. The kind of testing and exploring he was talking about may need to happen in a classroom. At the lunch table and back on the second floor in the evening, the focus and intensity of the most provocative classroom questioning is vitiated by time, by the presence of people who were not in the classroom, by the other events of the day, even by fatigue.

I was struck by this idea of the futility of recapturing the moments of real meeting of mind and idea, when a student spoke of "the right kind of class" as being one in which "something new is being created." This sounded like a rather wistful hope, and I asked him what he meant. He spoke of a special full-year course for students taking part in a national model United Nations session at the end of the year. The course subject in the preceding year had been Russia, and the twenty students involved were to represent that country in the model session. The special value of this, the new thing created, seemed to be the fact that the course was for a special set of students, with special interests and needs in the subject. It was not part of a scheme or catalogue. It was for them, and what they did with it mattered to them. The students involved insisted that what they did was a great deal more important than the fact that there were only twenty students in it. They, along with other students, may have been quick to recognize the problems of learning in the midst of the numbers game, but cutting down the numbers did not necessarily bring the creative encounter they thought would be so beneficial. On various campuses some students spoke of getting permission to enter graduate seminars. One, speaking for a number who had had this experience, said, "The trouble was, the grad students were so careful to be *mature!* There were five of us, and eight of them, and would they be wary! The professor would frown and they would look scared, as if the professor were going to say, 'Now *you're* a graduate student—don't be naïve and easily refuted.' "

The appreciation for the experience of "creating something new," however this theme was expressed, remains vividly in my mind long after these conversations. Perhaps this student spoke as well as any for those eager for the kind of encounter with a professor that was a meeting of two individuals, or at least of two thinking, interacting minds: "This man's in the international relations department. But the course isn't cut and dried. He, and it— the course—probe inside you. He'll ask us questions and make us think out answers on the basis of the whole pile of things we've read for the course. You come out confused, but *it's the kind of confusion you don't discard at the classroom door.* It's the kind of confusion you wrestle with all night, and you end up with a decision on what you believe in the morning."

12

"They," the Administrators

One of the oldest psychiatry jokes is the one about the doctor who says there is real progress once his patient begins to know just who *they* are. A mysterious, powerful, often sinister and abstract "they" sits heavily and often conveniently in the minds of a good many college students when they have any thought about who is "really running" their college. "They" is a cluster of perceptions of trustees, chancellor, president, president's staff, and deans, which lends itself to satisfying explosions and simple explanations about the way things are on the campus. "The administration" is a convenient answer to "Who are *they?*"

Once a student has any relationship with an individual administrator, whether he be a personnel dean or a member of the president's staff, or even the president himself, the "they" of "the administration" immediately breaks down. This does not mean that students find that to know an administrator is automatically to love him. It simply suggests that the less relationship students have with anyone involved in the elaborate structure which is actual "administration" on a campus, then the more easily are they lost in generalizations and resistances about "the administration." The vague, all-embracing "they" as applied to "the administration" is usually on the lips of a frustrated student who has no relationship with any adult on campus. To a student who is fiercely dedicated to a particular cause or concern, "they" become a single, blocking force working against his personal crusade.

This study showed that one of the most important contributions of the dean of students and his staff was to relate the student to "the administration," to give him some understanding of the college or university, and to allow him to think and work with representatives of "the administration" in a way that seemed to make sense to him and to the university.

Sometimes it was clear just who "they" were. One student was talking about what he thought was the apprehensive and even repressive attitude on the part of the president and his staff toward student political and social action: "The philosophy runs on about a responsible citizen and a responsible world and a widening universe and all, but everything you do is hampered. The administration is really torn between the German idea of educating, where the students aren't expected to know anything except their subjects, and the Jeffersonian idea of developing the individual. . . ." Since this student felt there was little enough interest in political and social concerns on that campus, he was all the more discouraged about "their" attitude. On another campus, the student who said, "They want to keep student activity under constraints. They say, 'How do we keep this at a minimum?' ", was speaking about the dean of students and his staff. "They" were for him what the president and his staff were for the first student.

When "They" Become Personalities

Once there was some relationship, some *person* with a face, a voice, and a pair of ears, "they" gave way to "him" or "her." This would most often be the dean of students or one of his staff. Sometimes it would be one of the president's staff, and sometimes the president himself. (One active fellow in student government and student activities said with pride, "We have better access to the president than most of the faculty and a lot of the deans!") Since it would most often be someone on the personnel staff, that person would have to be ready to put on and wear the projections of the most bristling student. But I was surprised at how little I saw of any administrator, particularly the deans in student personnel work, having to carry the ogre image attributed to him as a person by angry students. Once somebody in the "they" was willing to talk *and listen*, then the way was open for some sharing of concerns, responsibilities, and effort. A number of students were quite used to this. "The student government can really *talk* to the administration around here. There's a tradition about this. A lot of these things are detail stuff, but they add up and do *mean* something. . . ." Others were just discovering it, through a new dean or a new student attitude, or both. "There's the 'that's nice' attitude we used to get from the administration. Now a student wouldn't walk out after hearing 'that's nice' from the dean. He'd stay and ask for more. They used to say they'd 'take it under consideration.' The students never said 'When?' Now when the dean of students says, 'We'll take it under consideration,' we feel confident he will. And *we're* in on the 'consideration!' "

On one campus where the *structure for relationship* between administrators and students was particularly developed, the student president spoke of occasional accusations that he and the people around him were being brainwashed by the dean or by "them." He did not seem especially worried about this, partly because it happened so seldom, and partly because so many students were involved in *the network of relationships* with student government, personnel deans, activities advisors, and other administrators that there were plenty of students to refute the brainwashing charge. "The excitement and satisfaction in student government, the relationships with people, causes, and concerns beyond the campus, all stemmed," said this student president, "from having progressive administrators like the dean of students. Those people's expectations are such that we perform along with those expectations." He spoke of the university's president as "listening with both ears—I mean he *listens*," and students around him spoke of the administration's including students in many meetings where important decisions were made.

I heard variations of this theme on other campuses, though it was more likely to be an individual administrator rather than a policy or a structure of relationships that seemed so important and helpful. "The administration's willingness to deal with students is amazing!" said one girl who was awed by the experience of give-and-take she had just had in a conference with a dean and the vice-president for academic affairs. "The new president has had a profound effect on student government and student attitudes," said another, reporting on the access student leaders had directly to the president. "There are a lot of channels—student-faculty committees—lots of relationships. You can walk in and talk to a dean or someone in the administration building and be heard and feel part of things," said another student warmly. On the campuses with these channels, these possibilities for relationships, there was a lot more student concern about everything—from lockout hours to segregated housing in town, from student government to Birmingham, Cuba, and the Congo. It is not that the relationships between administrators and students led to these particular concerns. It is simply that some students felt themselves to be in an atmosphere of fairly easy exchange with some key adults on campus, and felt that they carried more responsibility as a member of their college or university and as people working out their own education. On such campuses, when the blowups come, the people involved will have more to go on, in meeting the problems and in making the experience somehow "educational" for everybody, rather than simply having to face a messy incident that has to be cleaned up.

How Do "They" See the University

The vision "they" have of what education should be, of what a college or university should be, and of what *this* particular college or university should be, had plenty to do with what students thought and did in and beyond the areas of political and social concern. If "they" believe that the community wear and tear is too great for students to have the experience of hearing controversial speakers, if "they" believe that students should be acted on but not consulted, if "they" believe that a student's exploration of the world and of himself are things he can be doing on his own time, or before college and after graduation, then the students on that campus are going to respond in some predictable ways. Rebellion, needling, minor sabotage on up to major explosions, often about minor things, are easy to set off and easier to publicize.

Then there is the equally possible response—the dull acceptance of a suspended childhood status across most of the campus, a habit of unconcern, an unreasoning caution, which students have absorbed from "them" without realizing it.

Many fine administrators speak up for free inquiry, for students to operate in freedom with responsibility. There is no question but that this commitment leads to as many or more problems than does the commitment to keep the lid on and keep the students' noses in their books or their beer mugs. The hope, as one dean put it, is that "the problems will be the right kind of problems, and that working on them will have some dignity." One of the universities in the study was beleaguered on many sides by forces that resented the institution's being "a university" in the sense its administrators could take seriously. One of its deans said, after the attacks were over and after many key administrators had resigned, "We told the students to be their own masters, find their own goals. The deans told them this and the president supported us. We believed it. We went on acting on this belief until the dictates of our society demanded that we pull in our horns. When you get older you have to be pragmatic. The kids don't understand this." He spoke of the tradition that moved himself and many of his colleagues: "We had all come from colleges and universities that had the liberalist tradition—the idea that one could examine *anything* and accept or reject it after examining. That was what we saw as a major purpose of a university. Plunk this concept in the middle of this community and start using the university as a *real* university and the community is horrified!"

This dean's view of the university was shared by many students. One said to me, "This used to be a kind of droopy place, kind of 'average kids' around—you know. Then some new people started coming in—students, deans, the president himself. We got this terrific dean of students. We couldn't figure out why he left his prestige job and came here. Kids would go to his house and ask him this. He'd say, 'You can be whatever you want to be around here.' He'd build us up. We saw money coming in from grants, new hot-shot faculty, a lot of life and discussion and controversy. Morale went up. They started talking about the Harvard of the

West, and they weren't kidding." The dean I was talking with spoke about this comment when I quoted it to him: "That's about right. We had here, I think, one of the best administrations I ever saw. It was exciting. The atmosphere was alive—why, last year you couldn't *stop* this university. It was really going places." He paused, thinking about the events of the past several months on the campus. "That's over now. Suddenly we find ourselves thinking about our families and our own careers."

This dean's comments are part of an ominous story, but they belong here, lest there be any impression that speaking up for freedom of inquiry and freedom of expression, plus some good personal relationships between students and administrators, will bring the new Athens on a college campus. The more intricate organization on his campus had impressed me so much and had won such great loyalty and participation of students that I remarked about it. He commented: "There's a mutual advisory system here that leads to a kind of sharing among students and administrators. We *work* with students. There's an atmosphere here for arriving at compromise. Sometimes this is assailed by students as the way the administration "takes students in." The procedure continues though, and the students seem to have respect for our good faith. But it's in an *attitude held in a series of experiences of working together.* It isn't in a "system" or constitution. Last year one of the local campus parties wanted the administration to define the area of student responsibility. . . ." (I had heard this plea on a number of other campuses, but not this one.) "I begged them not to ask for this and not to make us do it. That would *limit* student responsibility and student government, not strengthen it. We make no attempt to delimit the reach of student influence. Of course the Regents have the final authority, but there are fifteen students on the Board of Control of the University. If you start overdefining student responsibility, you start limiting it." This would sound different on different campuses and to different hearers. But on this campus it made evident sense.

Finally, those who make up the "they" have to face the probability of continued eruptions on campus and in the community, once students and faculty and administrators start playing seriously in the exploration of appropriate meanings for "freedom" in a university. The world presents enough real issues to permeate the campus and demand some kind of human response that the most compassionate, Socratic administration is still going to have its irresponsible students sometimes go wild and its responsible ones revile the deans as die-hards of the status quo. Its colleagues may assail it for letting students get out of hand, its community may attack it for its "permissiveness" and "softness," while on the campus even apathetic students may assault it for its "rigidity" and "coldness." It is then that the echo of the dean's hopeful words are needed: "These problems go with what a university needs to be doing, to be *being*, and no matter how harrowing they are, they are far more respectable problems than those old-time ones about rooting out the illegal drinkers from the backs of cars."

13

Out of the New Ferment

The new ferment, new in relation to so much we heard and saw of the college generation of the 1950s, did not begin yesterday morning. It was clearly visible in lively form on some campuses in 1962 or earlier. Specialists in social history, student counseling, sociology, psychology, as well as their occasional accompanying "sweeping generalizers," are seeking causes, trends, explanations, solutions, and schemes that "explain" this new ferment. But the new ferment itself includes many experiences and feelings and kinds of behavior. When the commentators "account for" whatever is new on the campuses, they may be accounting for a rising concern for political realities or for explosions of lawless student agitation, for a new maturity of social vision or for an ugly rebelliousness on the campus.

My own encounters with the students I met on this adventure make me far less eager to paint portraits and supply explanations than I might have been before I set out on it. And these encounters add up to impressions and speculations that are very different from any I had beforehand. Maybe the most satisfying explanations and generalizations live farthest from the complicated realities of campus and student. Yet, those who are in the midst of these complicated realities—the professors, the deans of students, and the students themselves—are often so immersed in living through them, in *being,* that they do not or cannot back away far enough from the experience to speculate on it, to make guesses about causes and directions. I have found that even the most astute and experienced deans of students, those who feel most in partnership with students in the adventure of education, are searching, not making pronouncements. Yet from those at the center of the experience we can find encounters, faces, and voices that give some reality to the speculations and interpretations of the visitors, investigators, and commentators. In their turn, these people can perhaps give some useful perspectives to those in the center of the experience.

A powerful influence in the new ferment on campus has surely been the intensity of support for the Civil Rights movement of American Negroes. The identification of white students with the struggle of American Negroes for rights, for freedom, for individual identity, and opportunity has been extraordinary in the experience of some students, including those of real influence on campus. It is easy to ask why it took so long for this identification to happen. Just as easy is the question of why it took the nation so long to bring the subject of Negro civil rights to the level of public concern and action we see today. The fact remains that, with apparent suddenness in the past few years, the subject has come to the center of the American public consciousness, and conscience, and with it has come the extraordinary identification of students with this cause. It seems to link up with some students' drives for their own individual rights, freedom, identity, and opportunity, which, when looked at logically, seem quite remote from the actual feelings, the actual struggle, of American Negroes in the Civil Rights struggle.

Yet, after hearing students talk, I have often thought that their own outreach, their feelings of wanting to throw off the "oppression" of adults and test their own powers, of wanting to be themselves and not someone else's image of themselves, of needing to count in the world's eyes (and their own) as individuals who matter—these feelings have found a powerful fellowship in what students see and hear in today's events and drives in the Civil Rights movement. It is not simply compassion, a desire to serve, a discovery of a cause. It seems to be an actual shared experience, a common struggle, strange as this may seem as one sits among a group of fairly affluent twenty-year-olds who are 3,000 miles from the day's recent headlines about Civil Rights.

A Taste of Responsibility, a Taste of Power

This "rights" identification has led to action, and this action has led to a whole new attitude toward campus life and toward student initiative and student power on the part of the young people involved in the action. College students were recognized as a major active force in some key struggles in the Civil Rights movement in the summer of 1963 and much more in the summer following. Thus the next academic year brought some campuses a handful or more of students with the experience of real responsibility and power under their belt. Back to college came young men and women who had organized themselves into effective groups to set up voter registration, who had designed and taken part in massive protests and demonstrations, who had established relationships between the races and between power groups in explosive communities, who had been beaten up by racists and "treated," as one young man put it, "to the experience of being a victim in a police state." Other students returned from a first encounter with tutoring deprived children, often Negroes, in desperately underprivileged neighborhoods, or from other service projects in which they felt they counted for something, were important to somebody.

Summer programs in Africa had an especially powerful impact on students I talked with, and here again the identification was working in a way similar to the identification with American Negroes. In some of the new African countries, the fact of an emerging race is joined in these students' feelings with the idea of an emerging nation, a new status, a new place in the sun, wrung from oppressors and heavily paid for. These are personal feelings to these students and not simply current events. What really animated these students returning from such experiences may have been quite different for each one, though I believe they had in common the identification with their own growing self-images. Some may have awakened most to the experience, and the power, of organized protest. Others may have been most moved by new relationships, either with familiar fellow workers in a common concern or with people they never would have met on any college campus.

As one professor said, "It's a case of 'how ya going to keep 'em down on the farm after they've seen' not Parree but Birmingham or the Boston slums." Students who had experienced the effectiveness, and the drama, of mass protest were ready to use these techniques on the campus for ends they saw as important, and this looked very different indeed from the rather scattered and emotional student protests of the past.

The New "Veterans"

There is going to be more of this kind of experience from which students will return, "from the world," after vacations and particularly after the summer, to a number of campuses. Such students are a powerful influence on the campus climate of the 1960s, and some of them are going to be involved in the campus-shaking, headline-making news to which some of us turn with apprehension and some of us turn with admiration.

It may seem odd to compare the veterans of World War II and today's "veterans" of community service, mass protests, or other kinds of identification with an intense world beyond the campus. Yet the two sets of "veterans" have some things in common. We used to hear a good deal about the veterans of World War II from 1946 to 1950, about the new seriousness they brought to the campus. With them came a moritorium on beanies and bonfires, football rallies, and Freshman Frolics. Those veterans seemed to seize onto their books and courses as if they were lifelines. The G.I. Bill gave the possibility of education to thousands who might never have walked onto a campus. To them and to others, education itself, meaning classes and books and credits and the degree, and perhaps the experiences within and surrounding these, was related to personal stability, a future beyond the joyful return home, alive, a way to a better life for themselves and their society than they had known in wartime's battles and terrible upheaval of their aftermath. While interest in building a new world was certainly a part of the life of these veterans, and while they came, in dwindling numbers, to meetings of initially exciting and idealistic groups like the American Veterans Committee, their main drive seemed to be a fierce personal encounter with the books. In those days, the professors were telling us how these veterans raised the standards of the kids who arrived from high school and mixed with their older and very different classmates, and we heard a lot about motivation, and serious purpose, and a new respect for education.

Today's new "veterans" of Selma and Ghana, of the New York slums and the Mississippi cellars, are bringing back to the campus a passionate identification with a crucial problem in our society and in the world itself. And amazingly enough, after hearing and reading for years about the futility of the individual in a complex and impersonal society, these young people feel they can be a part of the solution of the problem that has awakened them to action on the front lines. This kind of "veteran" is not returning with the feeling of entering the desperately won sanctuary of books, classes, ideas, and encounters with "education." He is looking around to see what can be done to enlist this "education," the experiences, the people, the organization of the institution itself in the solution of the problem. For such as he, the dramatic reality is off campus. For the "old" veterans of World War II, the reality, precious if not dramatic, was on campus, no matter how vivid the memories of wartime experiences. They rejoiced that the war was over. The new "veterans" see themselves in a "war" that has just begun.

The old veterans delighted their elders by their zeal for studies. The new veterans disconcert their elders by their zeal for demonstrations. And many of them have shown more than zeal: They have learned how to demonstrate, to protest, to rally a crowd, to organize a movement, sometimes even to put their opponents against the wall. These techniques look a little different on a college campus than they may have looked on the street before an Alabama courthouse. College administrators have been quick to say that the situations are different, that the campus is not the place for this kind of organized pressure. Some have spoken up with conviction for the very fact of a university's commitment to rational discourse as being reason enough for students to seek other styles and approaches from those used in the streets. Nevertheless, such college leaders often find themselves cast by their "new veteran" students in the role of a Governor Wallace or a Bull Connor. This may be infuriating as well as unfair, but it is happening, and many a dean of students or college president is being cornered into fighting his way out of such a role.

One final comparison between the two sets of veterans: The 1946–1950 veterans were not rallying their classmates to the cause of studying. They were simply studying as individuals and providing some competition and some example in the process. Today's "veterans" are vigorously rallying *their* classmates to their cause of concern or protest, service, or demonstration. Their efforts can be exploited by the whole range of noisemakers from self-styled revolutionaries or free-riding sports on an antiauthority spree. They can also evoke the most intense and admirable idealism. Just who will control the leadership and point the direction of the new ferment is a reverberating question on campuses today. And with it comes the immediate action question to professors, deans, administrators, and students themselves: How can the campus community draw out the lost constructive forces in the ferment to make the campus "education" and its contribution to society the more searching and relevant?

Bringing "Reality" to the Campus

Student experiences in Mississippi and Uganda are not the only realities being brought back to the campus. The sudden and mushrooming phenomenon of the teach-in is a new and exciting addition to the campus ferment. There have always been college professors who were trying to "bring reality to the campus," and often it was the exasperation of just such professors in the 1950s that brought us the portraits of the silent note takers who kept the off-campus world not only at arm's length but also at campus-wall's length. There were plenty of national and world problems worth wracking a campus about in the 1950s. As one looks back only a few years, it is hard to imagine a teach-in on the subject of Korea or McCarthyism on most campuses. What we are told of that student generation suggests that there would have been few student listeners. Or would there have been? Might not there have been a wave of excitement, and interest, and appreciation among students if some professors had tried just such a dramatic experiment in, say, 1954? Haven't students always been fascinated at their professors' out-of-class opinions, beliefs, and commitments? We can talk about the 1950s only with what-ifs. In the sixties it is students who have agitated most for an awakening to realities in the society, at least to those realities that they seized as emotionally and psychologically their own. The professors who were making pleas for this kind of identification were scattered about our colleges and universities, though I heard very little about them in my visits.

Today's most "awakened" students prefer to see themselves as the initiators, the discoverers, the creators of movements, and the leaders to compassion and service and action among their own generation. Now come the professors and the teach-ins, with students suddenly listening, far into the night. United States policy in Vietnam and in the Dominican Republic was the launching pad for the teach-ins, and soon the professors were hitting the headlines and the students were paying attention. Their attitude continues to be one of delight that the professors are suddenly awake to the world. Professors smile, or burn, at this interpretation. Yet, until very recently, the most repeated and publicized "campus attitude" seemed to be the students' impatience or contempt for the fence-sitting professor. The teach-ins seem to give evidence that the professors are shaken enough by world events that they must join the new ferment as intellectual, vocal leaders, and not simply as occasional fellow picketers. Nobody claims that an all-night teach-in is going to usher in a revelation on any campus. But the excitement and drama of some of the teach-ins, and students' response to them, show something more than that students have discovered a new way to avoid paying attention to their studies.

The college or university classroom that was relevant to society's current intensities and to students' awareness of them has not been often reported on by students in the past few years, to put it mildly. Surely the drama and the extra-classroom aspect of the teach-in carries more meaning to many students than all but the most powerful classroom experience. This is not to ignore the power of the best kind of classroom experience in which there is a real dialogue, with individuals thinking and listening, colliding and sharing. Until there are a lot more of these, the mass aspect of the teach-in can bring a sense of seriousness and size and fellowship, as well as excitement, that can be educationally vital to students, and this vitality is around many campuses now.

More important, the most seriously considered of the teach-ins, like the most seriously considered student efforts to express their impatience with a futile and juvenile studenthood and their concern and idealism about facing their society's problems, are making life on some campuses more relevant to the world. The student's sense of his role and the college teacher's sense of his may be much changed by the events that make up the new ferment on campus, and the signs are pointing to this already. I think the experience of a college or university education in *all* its aspects—not just in its outside experiences, all-night meetings, and occasional picketings—will become more important to students and to the society as a result of the new ferment.

The Academic Life

There is increasingly high-powered academic activity for students in colleges and universities today. How can students seek out and act out a sense of relatedness to the society's problems and explosions and still meet these intensified academic challenges? Or are the politically and socially concerned ones barely passing while the apathetic ones make Phi Beta Kappa? A consuming interest and ambition in academic achievement could take a student away from concerns, let alone involvement, in political and social realities beyond the campus. For some of the most thoughtful and socially minded students, the active and intelligent use of their minds along with the post-Sputnik intensifying of academic challenge in schools and colleges could lead to more interest in and more relationship with political and social concerns. The argument is that if students are made to use their minds more, then those minds will work more astutely on the issues of the day than they would have in the pre-Sputnik aca-

demic climate. This argument is less and less impressive the more
one sees and hears of college courses and programs that are
harder without being more genuinely intelligent, which take up
more time but do not touch the individual, reflective mind any
more than the pre-Sputnik courses did.

Colleges are not automatically stimulating desirable interests
and attitudes on political and social matters simply because
courses require "better preparation" and because college admis-
sions officers are more impressed with the current level of test
scores than they were a few years ago.

I met students in this study who were giving so much of themselves to their own kinds of political and social action that they
were having to drop courses, plan an extra year to graduate, or
even flunk out. For some of these, the academic side of college
was getting more and more remote. If they stayed in college, they
would be trying to cope with their academic work with a few
fingers of their left hands. The practical thing to do for them
would be to cope as well as they could with the academic demands
necessary for the degree, and for some next step after graduation.
But the real drive, energy, and concern is, as one young woman
put it, "not just in a different world from the campus's world, but
on what seems sometimes like a different planet." I suspect there
are many, many students like these who have given up ever finding
anything in the curriculum that relates to what they can care about
personally. They are not just looking for ideas with which to
identify. Some seem to be looking for an understanding about the
world they see beyond the campus. More want a sense of actually
"doing something" in the world, even if this "doing" is a new kind
of talk, or a gesture, a burst of emotion, or a temporary escape
from what seems to them the irrelevance of their campus education. And they take seriously the reality of their experience in the
summer, or in vacation time, or even in a few borrowed hours of a
direct encounter with issues and problems. The "world" is influencing such students as these, and perhaps equally strongly but
quite differently, a college curriculum and a set of campus activities which seem pointless. This is the dominant negative factor
in the new ferment.

The college dropout, watching his campus friends from the

viewpoint of the barricades in Selma, wonders how they can be so blind, so childish, and so unrelated to the driving issues of the day. And, on the other hand, it is not hard to find the student who thinks the fellow on the barricade is an impractical nut, and that even the best of the campus activists are deluding themselves about "doing something" that matters, even if he cannot actually attack the quality and sincerity of their concern. There remain what I think of as the important majority of the students who have already awakened or are awakening to concern. They look at the world and they look at the experiences and activities and material of their college education, and they are increasingly concerned about why the world and the campus seem to have no relation to each other at all.

There has been sobering and useful attention finally paid in recent months to the problems of giantism, massive classes watching a taped lecture by a professor whom they will never see and who will never see them. But irrelevance and frustration are possible on a campus of 400 as well as one of 40,000, if nothing that goes on seems to students to be "about" anything real that they see and care about in the exploding world beyond the gothic and grass. On the giant campuses and on the supposedly individual-minded small ones, the world and "education" need to have something to do with each other, and conversation about this relationship needs to go on between the generations and among the most thoughtful and caring members of the generations.

More than Just a Hope

A new relevance, a new seriousness about the world and what an individual can do in it and for it, will, I believe, come out of the new ferment. There will be more campus explosions that look, and may be, foolish and irrelevant to the issues they are supposed to be about. And there will be more explosions on issues that don't seem to be worth fighting for at all. Headlines and television screens and political slogans from Right, Left, and Center sing the word "freedom." The events which for many students make up the major drama of the nation have at their center a great mass of

Americans whose freedom and whose rights have been denied. Add this to the usual and normal reaching out for independence and selfhood in eighteen to twenty-two-year-olds, and there *is* indeed something new—and something complicated, for good or ill, for college campuses. It may bring a new kind of responsibility or a new kind of chaos on campuses, but it is way beyond the patronizing philosophy of "kids will be kids."

As I talked with students who were thinking seriously about political and social problems, it seemed a real hope that the more astute and mature of them who were suddenly aroused to the idea of freedom denied would tend more and more to focus on the problem in their own country, even their own community, rather than the translation of it into terms of "my personal rights" having to do with a traffic violation, dorm hours, or the dean's handling of a drinking problem. The colleges are asking a lot of students to expect them to discriminate between real issues and post-adolescent rebellions. Yet they need to ask just this. And from what I heard on these campuses, many students themselves are asking this, and are asking it with vigor, and idealism, and dedication that could promise much for our colleges and our nation.

The College Student Personnel Institute

The College Student Personnel Institute, for whom this study was made, is a privately supported organization working with both public and private colleges and universities.

The Institute which is now located in Claremont, California, was started in 1930 and incorporated in 1937 as a nonprofit educational association of member colleges and sponsor members. Each member institution appoints a representative to the Academic Council. The Council's chairman and chairman-elect are ex officio members of the Board of Directors, other directors are elected by the sponsor members.

Services

The Institute offers the following services to education:

Maintains the Joseph G. Prosser Library, an outstanding special library of books, pamphlets and research materials on all phases of student personnel

Serves as a clearing house of information for 55 member colleges and universities through annual conferences, consultant service and publication of bulletins and bibliographies

Plans and conducts research projects

Conducts a graduate study and internship program in college student personnel work jointly with Claremont Graduate School

Operates a counseling center to help individuals through professional educational and vocational counseling and to provide a laboratory for internship training

A national information service (1965) which includes abstracting relevant articles in fifty periodicals

Board of Directors, 1964–1965

GEORGE D. JAGELS, President
MRS. ARTHUR HANISCH, Vice President
MRS. HOMER CROTTY, Secretary
HUGH F. COLVIN, Treasurer
HELEN FISK, Assistant Secretary-Treasurer
DR. BYRON H. ATKINSON, Chairman, Academic Council
DR. JOHN C. CLEVENGER, Chairman-elect, Academic Council
ARTHUR L. CROWE, JR.
WINIFRED HAUSAM
MRS. JAMES E. MACMURRAY
DEXTER S. PADDOCK
MRS. MAX THOMPSON
GEORGE H. WHITNEY

Staff

DR. JOHN J. WITTICH, Executive Director
DR. JONATHAN R. WARREN, Director of Counseling and Research
MRS. MARY S. SAMSON, Institute Associate
MRS. JEAN HARD, Librarian

HELEN FISK, Editorial Consultant

Advisory Committee

DR. W. H. COWLEY
    David Jacks Professor of Higher Education
    Stanford University
DR. SAMUEL GOULD
    President, State University of New York
    Albany, New York
DR. T. R. MCCONNELL
    Professor of Education and Director,
    Center for the Study of Higher Education
    University of California, Berkeley
DR. RALPH TYLER
    Director, Center for Advanced Study in the
        Behavioral Sciences
    Stanford, California

Dr. Robert J. Wert
  Vice Provost and Dean of Undergraduate Education
  Stanford University
Dr. E. G. Williamson
  Dean of Students
  University of Minnesota

Affiliations

The Institute holds an associated organization membership in the American Council on Education. It is an affiliate member of the National Council of Student Personnel Associations, and an associate member of the Western College Association.

Index